MEANINGLESS SENSE TOO!

501 meaningless answers to 501 meaningless questions about meaningless things that don't make any sense at all and who in the world cares?

Written by Gary Gazlay

Published by BookLocker.com, Inc., Bradenton, Florida.

Printed in the United States of America.

None of the statements in this book are meant to make any sense whatsoever, and, if by chance, one of them makes sense it was purely by accident. The statements are not truth or words to live by. They are just words from a mind of someone who is often perplexed by the sheer emotion of subjugated values not determined to be valid by anyone who ever presumed to care about anything plausible. Finally, the sentences are not designed to be grammatically correct, whatever that means.

BookLocker.com, Inc.
2014

First Edition

DISCLAIMER

This book details the author's personal experiences with and opinions about meaningless humor. The author is not a licensed therapist, psychiatrist or psychologist.

The author and publisher are providing this book and its contents on an "as is" basis and make no representations or warranties of any kind with respect to this book or its contents. The author and publisher disclaim all such representations and warranties, including for example warranties of merchantability and personal advice for a particular purpose. In addition, the author and publisher do not represent or warrant that the information accessible via this book is accurate, complete or current.

The statements made about products and services have not been evaluated by the United States government. Please consult with your own legal or accounting professional regarding the suggestions and recommendations made in this book.

Except as specifically stated in this book, neither the author or publisher, nor any authors, contributors, or other representatives will be liable for damages arising out of or in connection with the use of this book. This is a comprehensive limitation of liability that applies to all damages of any kind, including (without limitation) compensatory; direct, indirect or consequential damages; loss of data, income or profit; loss of or damage to property and claims of third parties.

You understand that this book is not intended as a substitute for consultation with a licensed medical, legal or accounting professional. Before you begin any change your lifestyle in any way, you will consult a licensed professional to ensure that you are doing what's best for your situation.

This book provides content related to meaningless topics. As such, use of this book implies your acceptance of this disclaimer.

Introduction

I have been making up sentences that didn't make any sense and using them in greeting cards for almost 40 years. My wife Betty always encouraged me to publish this "craziness" for others to read and possibly give them the opportunity to chuckle. She is my best friend, and is the reason my first book *Meaningless Sense* was published in October 2008.

Betty gave me the idea for another book, *"Meaningless Sense Too!"* She shared with me her thoughts concerning what it would like for two people to engage in a "meaningless sense" conversion.

It is also my hope that the student's that I instruct will be challenged to properly use the vocabulary in this book as they lookup the contextual meaning of the "new" words that they read.

When to use *"Meaningless Sense Too!"*

When your brain needs to exercise!
When you want to exercise another person's brain!
When you need to laugh!
When you don't want to laugh!
When you want to try to make someone laugh!
When you really want to irritate someone!
When you want to confuse someone who is trying to impress you!
When you want to confuse yourself!
When you can't find anything else to read!
When you can't fall asleep!
When you want to make someone fall asleep!

How to read *"Meaningless Sense Too!"*

Read the book to yourself using different voices.
Ask a family member to read the book with you.
Ask a friend to read the book with you.
Find a person with multiple personalities to read the book to you.
Let a *Text to Speech* character read the book to you.

Suggestions for if you find it difficult to laugh?

Pick another time of the day to read *"Meaningless Sense Too!"*
Try reading the statements backwards.
Try letting someone read to you in a high-pitched voice.
Find someone to read *"Meaningless Sense Too!"* back to you in a foreign language.

Disclaimers

None of the *"Meaningless Sense Too!"* statements in this book are meant to make any sense what so ever and if by chance one of them makes sense in was by pure accident.

The *"Meaningless Sense Too!"* statements are not truth or words to live by. They are just words from a mind of someone who is often perplexed by the precipitous emotion of subjugated values not determined to be valid by anyone who ever presumed to care about anything plausible.

The sentences are not designed to be grammatically correct or what ever that means in light of all things that should not have been stated in the first place.

Dedicated to:

My wife Betty, who for over 32 years has loved me even though most of the time I have searched for the encouraging reflections of my need to dispel compelling insanity.

Special thanks to:

My family and friends, who after reading this book will undoubtedly, disavow any knowledge or recollection of the existence of a creature that is most of the time known as Gary Gazlay.

Table of Contents

"Meaningless Sense Too!" is divided into **Sessions**.

Man thinks himself wise until God shows him his folly

Session 1

"The inherit risk of unassuming contemplations"

When is unregulated gossip preferred over fabricated unconcealed recollections? (1)

When those who refuse to talk to trees that do not have feelings too understand the reasoning behind a particular outcome. (2)

Why is the inability to reason without arguing a sought after trait by those individuals who sing to the stars on darkened nights? (3)

Because persuasive words will never persevere in a climate of endless change and cloudless days of thunder. (4)

Is desired advice from anyone who admonishes uncertain indecision taken lightly by those who often fish without a hook? (5)

Only when possible problems are created from the knowledge that a crow will eat cat food from a dog bowl if it is left unattended under a large bush that looks like a tree. (6)

Will a person who tries to outdo anyone who does not care, waste away their life trying to find out why a three legged dog can run faster than a human with shoes that do not match? (7)

Yes, if the person is striving for what is best even though knowing that when a cow sometimes forgets to moo that this action might lead to nonconformity that cannot be suppressed by intimidation. (8)

Do people seldom wonder why no one gives a hoot about problems that do not really concern others who are trapped by the tormented dreams of birds that do not fly? (9)

When they realize it is a daunting task to speak in a tone that is a higher pitch than any animal or canine could even hear. (10)

Why are talents sometimes never used where it is advantageous for everyone to seek shelter from nonprofessional manipulators? (11)

Because completing a task on time is always more important then giving a task to someone who will never complete a complex puzzle that is advantageous to the stability of all things never thought of. (12)

Is success only found when the inner self strives to be greater than the greatness that is discovered by those who never gaze upon uncontrolled superlatives? (13)

Yes, when it possible to really define a person who is incapable of sustaining a conversation void of symmetrical animosity. (14)

Can a good night's sleep best be found when a person tries skillfully to terminate their snoring abnormality during the hours of darkness hidden by light? (15)

No, and they will find that trying to impress the intellect of those with less, will drive someone to the brink of paying for advice that is already accounted for. (16)

It is impossible to walk in the shoes of anyone who has not known how to run with exposed feet on a bed of sand spurs at a crowded beach. (17)

A better question might be "Is it always difficult task to find a reason why you will never find a flea living on a tick that's stuck on a cat that acts like a dog?" (18)

Will the newness of nothing old await anyone who will attempt to irritate the feelings of a repugnant extremist with an attitude? (19)

This can take place only when all possibilities that can be possessed by unconventional scorn live in awe of demented disgrace. (20)

Does only fruit that has been picked by hand taste better than vegetables selected by a machine that does not speak with integrity? (21)

I don't know, unless you are speaking of an unspoken expression that must never be articulated in the company of those who never try not to find equitable illusiveness. (22)

Can undertakings completed in a timely manner present a clear representation to the world of the solidarity between truth and fictitious jabberwocky? (23)

It is believed this can only take place when inflexibility is seldom sought after by anyone who aspires to elevate themselves to positions of undeserved impartiality. (24)

Is finding a purpose to pursue anything only possible when the improbability of despondent compatibility is determined to crush any resemblance of inexperienced spectators? (25)

Only when people who are seldom home on Tuesday nights concern themselves with anyone who invites others to dinner on a day exempt from inattentive adulation. (26)

When the light goes out on the inside of a vacant mind should a person ever take for granted that the wind sometimes blows through trees that have no leaves? (27)

If the person who whispers in the dark and howls at the moon is never allowed to wallow in a sea of self-pity that flows from a river without water. (28)

Could always being right when never being wrong be the explanation why some people decide not to reason? (29)

No, because a pessimistic go-between that tries to determine the reason a clock ticks and a duck squawks will eventually come to the conclusion that vaporous merriment is not contagious. (30)

Why is it sometimes difficult to forget those things that are seldom forgotten most regularly? (31)

Because seriousness endeavors that cannot be restrained are usually neglected. (32)

Can unrealistic disputed schemes continuously be jeopardized by naive relationships? (33.)

Sure, when those whose plausible deniability is detained by unforeseen probabilities. (34)

Is it true that hostile indifference can never be achieved by sympathetic remunerations? (35)

This question can only be answered when bewildering opinions never confound authentic compromise. (36)

Should sequential proclamations ever be allowed to suppress imprudent candor? (37)

Yes, when fragile disgust is never allowed to contradict the manifestations of cowardly intentions. (38)

When should animosity admonish antagonistic adoration? (39)

When harmonious assertions are never allowed to guide the incompetence of depreciated judgments. (40)

Is succinct brevity seldom achieved when obtained by sophisticated trepidation? (41)

The answer to this question will only be determined when boredom that is proclaimed in jest is allowed to revise the unemotional inflexibility of nothing changed. (42)

Why does infrequent dissemination of isolated malevolence often cause confusion in the lives of those who always strive to seek the purpose of retrospective meekness? (43)

It is because the concurrent coexistence is comparative only to the blatant transmissions of superficial discussions. (44)

Why is vanity sometimes discovered hidden inside the necessity of melancholy contentment? (45)

Because ridicule often resides in the realm of acknowledged predetermined resentments. (46)

Does the contrite recognition of subdued imperfections often cause disillusionment among those who seek predictive provocations of mistrust? (47)

Only when unconditional opportunities are awaited by those who refuse to manipulate informal interventions. (48)

Why does resistance to despicable contradictions often lead to the confusion of symbolic sensationalism? (49)

This is because momentary expedience is occasionally preferred over temporary inconsistency. (50)

Why does dishonesty that immerses itself in subdued conceit often misrepresent the intent of others who shun humility? (51)

The reason for this is that when a person always strives for perfection, a need usually arises to contemplate the necessity to affirm others. (52)

Do those who search for plausible dignity often resent probable denial? (53)

Only when thoughts made in silence occasionally fail to speak with absolute contentment. (54)

Why are restrained stubborn inhibitions difficult habits to maintain with remorse? (55)

Because individuals always plan for the best even if though the worst memory is detained by those who must search for restful habitations. (56)

Why must specific discretionary fixations never be allowed to dominate disinterested caricatures? (57)

Because systematic equalizations often fail to achieve the success needed to initiate intentional annoyances. (58)

Why is inadequate incompetence sometimes deemed incomplete by misrepresented distractions? (59)

Because abstract reasoning that is deprived of speculative principles will often fail in its attempt to circumvent speculative independence. (60)

Will restraint that is tempered by remorseful exuberance ever find contentment in obstinate apprehensions? (61)

Yes, because hopelessness that is not defined by disputes will lead it to controversial innuendoes that are not based upon courageous obscurities found in the necessity of unwanted functionality. (62)

Why must pundits continually ponder the presumptions of proper procedures that often persuade others to proceed without any regard to verified pretense? (63)

I guess it is caused by their contentment for presumptions that often avoids a regret that confines itself to a lifetime of erroneous pleasantness. (64)

Sooner or latter when do all things deteriorate into the oblivion of euphoric metamorphosis? (65)

When endless despicable condescension hides behind the dreary dark shadows of contemptuous complements. (66)

Why is extravagant abundance searched for but never found in the deterioration of dialectic disillusionment? (67)

It is caused by ordinary halfhearted allegorical negligence that occasionally confuses those who refuse to listen to simplistic adjudications. (68)

When are critical insights determined to be necessary for the survival of ethics not yet believed to exist? (69)

Only on Wednesdays, when repressed sorrows often ponder the mournful bliss of adoring reverence. (70)

Why must some people seek the humorousness hidden within benign sentimental aspirations that confront sensible ambitions? (71)

Because waiting in the space of time sometimes not yet determined, leaves a psychological imprint of precise miscalculations. (72)

Do irrational inaccuracies usually unfold into a menagerie of false innuendoes not to be believed? (73)

They can if the regrets that often precede optimistic politeness attempt to fundamentally control uncontrollable outspoken humiliations. (74)

Why is it preposterous to assume that nothing is ever followed to the degree in which it was first presumed inevitable? (75)

Because trying to alleviate the need to gravitate towards the repugnant demoralization of obstructive impediments, is an easy task for all those who must always strive to be near but not too far. (76)

When should misleading auspicious distractions become a substitute for premeditated politeness? (77)

When unhappy faces occasionally hide the necessity to resemble moments borrowed from perilous bewilderment. (78)

Why must political correctness always be engaged with an authentic enthusiastic desire to confound the basic truth that is restrained by the same views that others seek? (79)

Because despite the best intentions, devotion to rational inclinations is best served when only left alone for as long as it takes. (80)

If ambitions only goal is to achieve the greatness of sensible intellect, will it always fall short in its desire to achieve the marvelous reverence of contemptible comparisons? (81)

It will, if an untamed aspiration is more challenging to envision than an attitude that strives to overpower the gravitational pull of contemptible whispers. (82)

When will an individual who contemplates the consequences of deceitful abstinence sometimes persuade others to join in the gracious praise of intentional futility? (83)

Usually, when undetermined perplexities resemble capricious whimpers that prohibit accumulated mischief. (84)

Can an impassioned barrier of deceit that is left alone by those who inherit habitual kindness, mesmerize the plausibility of symbolic reasoning? (85)

Yes it can, if significant unpopular philosophies generated from deep within a hardened heart attract individuals who long for outspoken complaints received in jest. (86)

How does unstoppable confidence hide from an onslaught of inconsistent enthusiasm? (87)

The reason for this is that some people prefer the apprehensive disapproval of foreboding gracefulness that is left abandoned in despair. (88)

Will unpleasant contradictions continuously prevail in an obscure world where nonexistent annoyances diminish when confronted by plausible resistance? (89)

It might, if disdainful stipulations compel others to continually misrepresent ridiculous coalitions. (90)

Why is the shameless disgrace of the nullification of abhorrent depravity an unwanted trait not visited by those who seek the purification of annoying absent-mindedness? (91)

An individual should constantly attempt to welcome visionaries even if immeasurable damage has been perpetrated on others through speculative enthusiasm. (92)

Must an allegation that acknowledges the achievements of harmonic congruencies ever be allowed to thrive in a sea of accommodated graciousness? (93)

No, it must not unless habitual familiarizations frequently persuade others to rethink their use of cultivated calculated cleverness. (94)

9

Why is compromising shrewdness so compelling when those who must always alter its truest form use it? (95)

The reason is that impatient dissatisfaction sometimes is manifested in the outward gestures of those who seek to capture the emerging regrets of anyone who lacks stupidity. (96)

Does impassioned fervor ever offer a freeing experience for those who must always verbalize the harmonious elegance of inconsistent slander? (97)

Yes, if noises heard from afar frequently care to listen to the reasons others choose not to believe. (98)

Who decided that scandalous intrigue is never reprimanded by anyone who declares to the world that nothing should ever be disapproved if left with others? (99)

Those who exam a heart for truth and forget to relinquish all authority to individuals who do not seek the reestablishment of uncultured elegance. (100)

Session 2

"Proactive contemplations of radical narratives"

Do those who scorn the methodical use of contrite relevance sometimes recollect residual residue? (101)

Never, unless beneficial adulation sometimes displays a ferocious desire to abstain from unwanted struggles of unfinished merriment. (102)

Why is an ego that spurns flattery mesmerized by pretense? (103)

The intention is that simulated inconsistencies are generally concealed from the complete view of anyone who escapes from the benefits of uplifting nuances. (104)

Can skillful research presume to always know more than those who fundamentally withdraw from fabricated despair? (105)

If it understands that to properly perform a duty with the right attitude requires an undetermined desire to strive for perfection that is only known by a few who anticipate compliments. (106)

Gary Gazlay

Why is hope that is not based upon varying degrees of polite expressiveness always confronted by the devotion to properly persuade affective superstitions? (107)

Because it is never impossible to rethink the substantive value of abnormal dilemmas that only exist in the minds of insinuated traditions. (108)

Will knowing when not to do what you know not what to do confuse even those who often retreat into the nonconformity of inherited traits? (109)

Yes it will, unless a toothless dog and a cat without whiskers have less in common with a skeptical procrastinator then with a suppressed agitator that looks like a crocodile. (110)

How is it possible for some people to never understand the complications that come from a hasty decision made by those who care not for homemade mush? (111)

The reason for this is that confounding the confused is essential when trying to intimidate those that are not even scared of armadillos that stare into oncoming headlights. (112)

Why are some people drawn to the light of souring possibilities, and some are content in settling for private considerations? (113)

Because people who always say what they mean and mean what they should have said, are incapable of flying a kite in the month of many memories. (114)

Why is waking up in the morning to the pleasant sounds of flowers that sing, an unusual occurrence for anyone to witness including a worm without wings? (115)

Some people believe that mystifying a disorganized person is crucial when attempting to frighten those who are not terrified of something that never really existed in the first place. (116)

Does it really matter to never give up on believing that seeing only the best in someone brings comfort to those who are trying to save a treasured fungus from ultimate destruction? (117)

It only matters if the spontaneity of any moment doesn't depend on the cessation of unjustified patterns of discouragement. (118)

Are contemptible qualifications often exhibited in the lives of those who shun the repulsive aversion to peculiar degradation? (119)

They are usually only exhibited when the disillusionment of despicable ideas confronts any system of knowledge that seeks to renounce the wisdom of competent ideas. (120)

Will truths that are often spoken with straightforwardness typically dissipate when confronted by unsolicited brevity? (121)

Only if a person who is never happy is content to be sad about anything that can be explained away by verbal neglect. (122)

Can an intelligent individual who must always avoid anyone who resents perfectionism, ever find true happiness searching for a token apology spoken with unbridled resentment? (123)

Not unless they understand that forgetting to forget is much harder to accomplish before attempting to conceptualize the hypothetical obscurities of condescending tolerance spoken in bitterness. (124)

Will an impulsive insensitive individual who is sometimes flustered by overpowering bewilderment attempt to transcend the postponement of unyielding shrewdness? (125)

Not until an individual who idolizes the respect of anyone who produces enthusiastic applause earnestly seeks the adulation of those who find worthy devotion useless. (126)

Will divulging a secret in confidence usually hamper the embellishment of belated esteem? (127)

Not unless profitability that attempts to disregard the futuristic exploits of promotional enterprises, respects the tenderness of anyone who embraces devotion to unwanted ideas. (128)

Should the encouragement of recommend support be allowed to promote the deliberation of unfavorable proclamations? (129)

Yes it should, if those who yearn for the recurring reflections of aggravated affections embrace the fondness for traditional afflictions. (130)

Does a cautious person who exhibits in their life a total lack of regard for the dissatisfaction with predictable hostility, often reminisce over the memories lost but not chosen in the forgotten past? (131)

Only when the thoroughness of tasteful thoughtfulness is appreciated by those who are attentive to the sensitivity of a blissful few. (132)

Why are a few tranquil moments often found occupying the space of least respect? (133)

Because the compensation for the adjustments of deceitful limitations allows individuals to refrain from divulging disgusting pleasantries with anyone who is enchanted by sudden unexpected predicaments. (134)

Is anyone really ever delighted when they seek the rewards of induced laughter? (135)

Only individuals who have discovered that expressionless immaturity can be an enchanting way to terminate the necessity to discontinue ritualistic formality. (136)

Is it wise to never scold anyone who must be reprimanded in front of others for actions that are cherished by those who respect undetermined consequences? (137)

It is only wise if the undetermined pretense of any situation is complicated by mere words of flamboyant conjectures. (138)

Should any momentary feeling of euphoria precede a desire to formulate concise characterizations of fearless impertinence? (139)

Only if the constant grading sound of proclaimed dissonance boggles the minds of those who choose not to listen to the scorched babbling of an intruder who is unannounced. (140)

Why is a person who always tries to intimidate others, like a virus that is brutalized by abrupt rudeness? (141)

Because distress caused by contemplating the need to exact restraint from what was avenged, never relieves anxiety. (142)

Is standing on basic principles usually appreciated by those who search for the provocative verification of benign ritualistic absurdities? (143)

No, it is only appreciated by individuals who are trying to restrict the necessity to withhold adulation from those less deprived of absolute genuineness that was undertaken in anger and hidden from the truths of suppressed jubilations. (144)

Why is the character of a person never really recognized until that individual is faced with the challenges of enchantments that are depreciated over a period of time that has not yet been determined by those who never initially cared? (145)

It is really never known because attempting to reason with a fool is like trying to reason with the attitude of someone who always neglects to express the truest form of deceit hidden in plain view from a world that is unreliable at best. (146)

Is duplicity in thought respected by persons who live a long life void of controversial confusion? (147)

It is usually respected through turmoil that is generated by captivating smiles that are regularly misinterpreted by the prolonged persistence of alluring fascinations, which were patterned after the counterfeit incantations of sequential encouragements. (148)

When attempting to determine the purpose of meaningful discussions, is it possible to focus on the perilous plight of disputable transformative persuasions? (149)

It is only possible when plausibility is sometimes hidden in the deceitfulness of those who attempt to personify a hidden desire to be appreciated for their congenial inept influences. (150)

Why do debatable debacles usually depict a need to mimic a fictitious form of fraudulent interdependence? (151)

It is usual because an individual who always presumes to know everything about anything is generally incapable of describing to anyone the theory behind the sustainable equivalence of all suitable exactness. (152)

Is it possible that authentication can only be confirmed when others attempt to approach the tangible contentions of significant persuasions? (153)

It is only possible if a person's well-mannered boldness is based upon a lack of confidence that is focused on a need for a personal ability to impart evasive competence that is ill humored at best. (154)

Do people who must always embrace the need to continually attempt to astound others with their ill-mannered skeptical intellects, usually end up surrounding themselves with friends who dabble in the ridiculous shortcomings of fragmented irritability? (155)

Yes, and especially during perilous times that always brings out the best in those who confront the dawning of a new life filled with the hope of isolation and obscurity. (156)

Why does living for the applause and validation from everyone usually develop in an individual a narcissist self-satisfied attitude that is void of any egotistical aptitude? (157)

Because composure to arbitrary obligations is an attribute only enforced by agreeable people. (158)

Can the execution of an intricate collaboration of obligatory reasoning be appeased by a reluctance to understand the perceptions of suitable opposition? (159)

They can be appeased when recorded amusements are determined suitable for the distribution of illusions that cannot be induced. (160)

Why should the theoretical collaborations of an objectionable utterance be confined to the suitable struggles of succinct ideals? (161)

The actual motive for this is that subtle immeasurable complaints sometimes manifest themselves in the accumulated pitfalls of cooperative convenience. (162)

Is it possible for every comprehensive compromise to find remorse in the conceit of those who qualify for objectionable compensations? (163)

Not unless the feeling of self-satisfaction is achieved by meager words of discarded importance that has been overlooked by those who possess disconcerting temperaments. (164)

Are the meticulous contemplations of bountiful thoughtfulness usually restricted by the simultaneous displeasure of commonplace classless individuals who are void of any conceit? (165)

It is never an appropriate action to conspire with a close friend who desires not to neglect the satisfaction of finding fault in those who are never antagonistic to anyone who earnestly communicates to others with any lack of distorted passion. (166)

Is it a good idea to always flee from a headstrong person who neglects the wishes of those who assume the limitless responsibilities of others that are often repressed by situational fortitude? (167)

It is only a good idea if someone who strives to betray the repression of old ideas will someday be rewarded by those who scheme to impart the endowment of superficial wisdom that is impoverished by misshaped distortions. (168)

Will a faint-hearted person who attempts to alter the authenticity of persuasive change, ever contend with others for the prominent role of positional dictatorial confirmation? (169)

Yes, if those individuals who understand that uncommon valor without ill-humored politeness will fade away into the oblivion of ill-tempered humility. (170)

Is it probable that a faultfinder can detract from the personal need to illegally transgress against someone who strives for the approval of those who manifest demented perfection? (171)

It is only possible if that person is confined to a life of demented kindness and shrinks from responsibilities that are predictable and yet comforting. (172)

Why do the memories of a lasting embrace always linger in the minds of persons who seek the affectionate nurture of unrefined enlightenment? (173)

It is because a delicate balance always exists between individuals who seek the refinement of habitual fragmentations and those who never strive to please anyone who should have become someone else. (174)

Does a feeling of overwhelming annihilation often permeate the air of those who emit a malevolent odor not yet discovered by individuals who eat beans? (175)

The treacherous attitude of those who seek the art of deceptive isolation always lurks in the shadow lands of obscurity concealed from anyone who refuses to judge, that which cannot be determined by a sense of smell. (176)

Why does bewilderment typically precede those who follow a path less traveled by anyone who seeks to eradicate the presence of any known liability? (177)

Because controversial questions that are deceptive in character often run away from the craftiness of bewildered misrepresentations that pretended to be an acquaintance. (178)

Should any lucid individual who attempts to proclaim to others the insufficient shortcomings of those who have neglected the adornment of obstinate corruption, triumph over the self-realization of corrupted depravity? (179)

Only if those lucid individuals understand that the satisfaction of demented confusion should frequently be used to illuminate the deceptive reputation of contradictory rebukes. (180)

Why do insufficient explanations often try to justify the need of a vagabond to resent the unsolicited recommendations of those individuals who oppose the necessity to abandon the pristine embellishments of blameless imperfections? (181)

It is because imperious challenges should never insist on rebuking the ignorant proportional disgrace of procrastinators who always finish their deliberations on time. (182)

Is it true that irrational hallucinations are often prevalent in the lives of those who attempt to charm the disgraceful exhibition of premeditated rejection? (183)

It is only true when discouragements that can be repudiated are found to amuse the negligent attitudes of individuals who refuse to acknowledge the stupidly of social contradictions. (184)

Should the tragic mockery of those who must always ridicule anyone who has risen above the hopelessness of discouraging desperation, ever be appreciated by someone who longs for the premature abandonment of picturesque desperation? (185)

Not unless a compassionate individual envisions that a lifetime filled with desolate isolation awaits the unsuspecting admirer who desires to be appreciated by those transparent personalities who are oblivious to systematic undeveloped discouragement. (186)

Will any nauseating conversational exchange of verbiage between two individuals of opposite extremes lead to the disillusionment of vicious unmerited approvals? (187)

No, because never wanting to change for the sake of needed change will usually change nothing but the intense desire to never change anything worth changing. (188)

Is it true that autocratic tyranny awaits nations who persist in degrading the eradication the attitudes of those persons who strive to cultivate the awareness of itemized chaotic gratitude? (189)

Only if there is an understanding that perceptive perceptions have no place in a society that occasionally attempts to defame individuals who must always masquerade their nauseating flare for unrestrained modesty in a labyrinth of bewildering compliments. (190)

Will difficulties regularly persist in the lives of those who consistently oppose the straightforward reasoning of an emissary that attempts to provoke someone who is incapable of interpreting the undisclosed messages behind insignificant discreet applause? (191)

No, because any person who lives a life full of discriminating inconsistency will always require the tools necessary to frustrate anyone who must never be chastised. (192)

Why is never quitting in the face of daunting obstacles, a trait exhibited only in the lives of heretics who will never be discovered searching for proportional deviations? (193)

It is because the repugnant frugality of deceitful backbiting is never intended to usurp the authority of those who were never in charge. (194)

When is tasteful disgrace a mirror image of impolite discrepancies that have been confused by tasteless perceptions? (195)

When kindness that is provoked by a lack of senseless humor is regarded with contempt by those individuals who never tried to understand the true nature of all things that have been rejected by a repugnant exchange of sobering ideas. (196)

Can a person who is reluctant to divulge a secret spoken in haste, ever be trusted to compensate anyone who has been discredited by impartial ramblings of the heart? (197)

Only when the caring individual attempts to dissuade the use of words that not only insult but delicately disclose the condemnation of deceptive enlightenment. (198)

Why does irreverent displeasure habitually permeate the minds of those who express a desire to propagate the objections of an obvious compromise in a presumed preponderance of undeserved belligerent mercy? (199)

Because intense devotion to cynical compulsive behavior is often misdiagnosed by improperly desensitized characters that pursue the questionable momentary accreditation of a few witless people. (200)

Session 3

"Maximum distaste of unprovoked ramblings"

In a senseless world full of the unannounced rumblings of unnecessary mammoth proportions, why are changes proclaimed by those who feel the urgency to make things that were not seen, visible to only those who have made the decision to not even attempt to delve into the remote possibilities of looking past the future? (201)

This is because nothing less is never less than anything at all unless things that are never seen can always be uncovered. (202)

Why does completing a task that originated out of an obligation to procrastinate, usually enhance the illustrious egos of those who never fail to interrupt a meeting scheduled on the wrong day? (203)

The reason is that compelling arguments need not be divisive if the intent of their desired meaning was useful for the time and place where mere words were not spoken with gestures hidden from the truth. (204)

Is authoritative control often embraced by persons who are least embarrassed by contrite skepticism spoken with an attitude of dubious wonderments? (205)

Authoritative control is embraced when those who always strive to interpret the illegitimate dispositions of decaying despotic injustices, misunderstand overbearing exuberance. (206)

Why do philanthropic apprehensions frequently permeate suspicious ramblings of an extremist who has ostracized those who accept the sacred traditions of exorbitant extremes? (207)

It is because monumental undertakings should only be attempted if there is a true sense of enthusiasm held by those who seek new ideas that were never completed. (208)

Why is the excursion into the realm of the unknown shortcomings of those who are dismayed, often hard to diagnose without the proper display of meaningful disrespect? (209)

Because properly performed responsibilities are never decreased by the seduction of cynical questions that have become monotonous by the reflection of complex answers. (210)

Why do endless days of slothful abandonment await those who properly avoid premature prosperity? (211)

The reason for this is that a simple minded person who continually partakes in the tendency to provoke heartfelt warmth of new ideas, should never be trusted by anyone who believes in the indecisive deception of repetitious stupidity. (212)

Is the gratification of the reassurance of a job well done, sometimes immersed in the complexities of intolerable amusement of laughter that is only funny to those who never care to recite a ridiculous riddle? (213)

Not unless defining the applicable moment to temporarily engage in a manipulative dialog of deceit, is often misinterpreted by those who search for the path of life that leads to the enlightenment of perfected acceptability. (214)

Should those who are usually impatient with any new ideas that were never void of compulsive obscurity, approve any obligation that becomes a liability? (215)

Not until the properly identified astonishment derives its influence from inconsistent persistence that is void of conscientious simple-mindedness. (216)

How does a conceited attitude that permeates the prideful arrogance of a pretentious remark, ever find reassurance in the lack of productivity that is concealed from the plain view of a self-centered person whose egotistical aura permeates the unconventional peculiarities of contented sheep? (217)

By searching for the simplistic complexity of adequate abnormalities that is often considered vain abnormal behavior by anyone who leisurely awaits the destruction of mundane prohibitions. (218)

Why are hidden emotions so regularly revealed in the lives of a choice few who seldom seek for senseless moments temporarily prolonged by the awkwardness of times best forgotten? (219)

Because they live for tomorrow only if tomorrow cannot be today. (220)

When is deviating from an unpredictable path ever an occasion to gloat over the demise of others who have rejected the depravity of inevitable ultimatums? (221)

When astonishment that confounds those who are dumfounded by the shock of false deception, resides in the cynical obscurities of influential boredom. (222)

Should a doodler ever be scrutinized for expressing a need to express thoughts that are not known by anyone who deserves to be left alone? (223)

Not unless the lethargic desensitization of an indecisive mind influenced the conscientiousness of anyone who desired to imitate the mannerisms of someone who fled the dullness of blissful gloom and despair. (224)

Can broken obligations normally sever the relationships of those closest to the intervals of impulsive enthusiasm? (225)

Possibly, if the premature unexpected enthusiasm for the relief of competent undertakings quiets the souls of those who attempt to enlighten the inner ears of everyone who is listening for the unashamed use of egotistical haughtiness. (226)

Is pretentious behavior that is often observed in the lives of those who radiate analytical boldness, usually hindered by the undetermined needs of nothing that really matters? (227)

Yes, if communities who are tastefully ignorant of the misappropriation of acceptable sophistication accept the outspoken discontent. (228)

Will unabashed emotional trickery ever take the place of supervisors who must procure the humiliation of acceptable rejections? (229)

Not until some folks live in the land of odd where nothing seems straight but narrow. (230)

Is to know what not to do always more important than not knowing what you should have done before you attempt to forget the things you were incapable of achieving? (231)

It is important only to the citizens who confuse those that vainly pursue the praise and esteem of enthusiastic resentments. (232)

Why may impartiality be impractical for someone who delights in supporting the uncontrolled joy in others that sometimes permeates from a grateful superficial debacle? (233)

It may be impractical because ordinary individuals who do not care for the enlightenment of captivating enchantments will one day disregard everybody who ignores the past. (234)

Why is ethical decency sometimes found in the lives of those who search for the misrepresentation of fundamental irregularities? (235)

Because it is best to never irritate someone who does not wish to be engaged in an intriguing conversation that will knowingly exacerbate an erroneous necessity to conform to the feelings of undefined acceptable standards. (236)

Why does a person avoid the views held by anyone who seeks to dominate the humane respectability of animals that only share their feelings with others who do not exist? (237)

Because neglecting to inaccurately interpret the exact time needed to institute an elaborate change in a direction, is only known by those who have met the one person who thinks that an individual exist who can correct the qualms of the unburdened masses. (238)

Why is stupidity that is cloaked in the immense reflections of derogatory remarks never present in the worthlessness of structural integrity mismanaged by inappropriate etiquette? (239)

Because to venture into the unknown frenzy of simulated apathy is an attribute that is better left for others who most always attempt to interpret the reason for evasive augmentative deliberations exhibited in the lives of those who are incapable of deciphering the hidden meaning behind lucid discloser. (240)

Can hopelessness that is imbedded in the hollowness of an underlying premise ever be revealed if the answers to questions yet to be determined are provoked by the limits of unbearable despair? (241)

Only if speculative augmentations are never allowed to overtake declarative embellishments proposed by collective abstract generalizations. (242)

Is it true that an individual must hope in today before tomorrow is not realized by sheer nothingness? (243)

Only when an unselfish attitude is the most desired trait exhibited in the complex lives of all entities that search for the surrealistic essence found only in the realm of repulsive generosity. (244)

27

Why does an overwhelming lack of excitement often accompany those who never attempt to uphold the names of illustrious nobility ignored in the annals of timeless persistence? (245)

This is attributed to the magnificence of picturesque splendor that can only be rewarded by creatures that possess the power to grasp the inevitability of promises proclaimed with a never-ending passion for uncompromising greatness. (246)

Can sentimental regards given during a gloomy situation undoubtedly lead to an increase in abrasive gratitude that does not necessarily reflect the frightful complaints of animosity uttered in complete silence? (247)

Only when the innocent babbling of incomplete hallucinations negates unaccounted responsibility. (248)

Will people who never make mistakes in their own empty minds that are filled with resounding echoes, someday challenge individuals who must manipulate others to complete an unnecessary task? (249)

Unyielding accidental annoyances will bring a smile to the face of someone who is dismayed by the apprehensions of unrelenting embarrassments and resounding echoes. (250)

Is antagonism usually embarrassed by animosity that can never be subdued by repugnant spurts of symmetrical torment? (251)

Not unless a genuine response to sincere insensitivity can repair the damage done to a relationship affected by the indecisive neglect of disturbing wholeness. (252)

Why is a sudden uncalled outburst of spontaneous creative negativity often unappreciated by those who spurn the unrealistic value of evasive extravagance? (253)

Because they believe that advice given by a person who desires to live a secluded obscure life will usually convey a wavering message of textual conformity to those who are endowed with innate simplistic thoughts. (254)

Why is unprovoked intentionality, thought to be a precise means of communication between anyone who holds to the steadfast inertia of strict superiority and an individual who believes in the complicated complexities of elaborate misrepresentation of heightened authenticity? (255)

Because there is an abundance of ultimate challenges that retreat from the humble life of a person whose life reflects the neglected attitudes of characteristic predetermined overtones of arrogant confidentiality. (256)

Is it the purpose of some individuals to encourage others to find resolution in the ongoing power that inhumane decency has over a wide range of views that are scattered throughout the four corners of a fabricated magnificent universe? (257)

Not unless they scoff at the exquisiteness of emulated provocation and will one day need to be restrained by those who least expect to be disturbed by hotheaded impetuous maniacs. (258)

Is the secret to pursuing a lifelong dream usually detected in the lives of those who are often weakened by the ridiculous claims of passive intimidation that reeks from a meaningless life that is always amused by whimsical inconstancy? (259)

The actual secret is hidden in the fact that wealth that is typically invested in the resources of depreciated funds will accumulate interest on the dividends that have been squandered on the portfolios of capital amassed by an insurmountable debt. (260)

Will environmental pollution that warms the enthusiastic outcry of everyone who feels the pain of a beloved earth yearning to be made whole, someday contaminate the purified scope of breathable air that has been contaminated by the confrontational impetuousness ozone layer of monolithic fabrications? (261)

Not unless any act of kindness is appreciated by those who care not to listen to the pleasant sounds of turkeys which seldom fly in the months of a year that does not have holidays. (262)

Why is prolific productivity often mishandled by anyone whom attempts to perform without a scowl of unimportance on a face that never smiles at failures unappreciated? (263)

Because impending doom awaits those exceptional individuals who race to a finish line that never existed in the future and could eventually dissipate in the newness of time least remembered. (264)

Why do persons who always complain when others quarrel, tend to disregard any whimsical occurrence that does not represent the real beliefs of a particular influence that was never appreciated in the first place? (265)

Because the type of person who refuses to catalog any refuse will usually continue to be honored by those who entertain spectators who must always create a disturbance that is incomprehensible to those without an abundance of common sense. (266)

Is it common for those individuals who must strive to speculate on the relative theories of ambiguous conjunctive analysis, to avoid any contact with a wanderer from a country far from the mainstream of speculative reasoning? (267)

Not unless a person who amasses an abundance of wealth squanders the perspective of indefinite wisdom that never assumes to postulate the need for unaccepted kindness. (268)

Why do the impersonal benevolent attitudes of others often reflect the need to consume a bountiful supply of hospitality that is unaffected by the changing perspective of authentic merriment? (269)

Because they exhibit talent that is void of any capacity to remember the significance of substantial obtrusiveness and will never achieve the respect that is always assumed by those who flee from counterfeit aptitudes of genuine repulsive warm-heartiness. (270)

Are mood swings an appreciated asset to an illustrious career that has departed from the realm of determined grander yet to be revealed? (271)

Unprovoked gossip will never replace the desire of others to degrade an influx of proprietary retaliations that are seldom directed towards anyone who propagates a message of simplistic occupational frustrations. (272)

Do those who often mistrust nonthreatening circumstantial verifications, sometimes make the assumption that the eventual collapse of society is due to prevalent undetermined issues? (273)

Yes, and the only difference between the hypothetical reasoning behind the circumference of a notable suggestion is usually unknown by those who make an honest effort not to disturb anyone who has an aptitude for uttering animated suggestions in secret. (274)

Why are individuals who must always taunt others usually void of any regret for the contributions made by a majority of their friends who were content to be left undisturbed in obscurity? (275)

They have not yet come to the realization that happiness often flees from the cloudiness of gloom that reflects the glossiness of withdrawn intemperance. (276)

Is progress usually measured by the significance of situational obstructions that are clearly marked for destruction by opposing agreements? (277)

They are normally measured when sudden atmospheric mood swings reveal an outward manifestation of a decaying inner immunization that cannot relate to the brilliant shimmer of options that must always correspond to speculative opinions. (278)

Is a grateful heart usually appreciative of obligations that have seldom been acknowledged by those who sneer at every mention of gratitude that is continuously provoked by those who never feel compelled to defend the splendor of bureaucratic importance? (279)

Not unless the greatness of revealed excellence is permanently manifested in the unfruitful display of displaced artificial affection. (280)

31

Will any individual who displays an attitude of indifference to those persons who always proclaim the sullen hypocrisy of inexorable occurrences, ever find happiness pursuing the frivolous pursuits that are never neglected? (281)

A bleak mundane life often awaits anyone who ignores individuals who must always pursue the exhilarating gloom of despair. (282)

When a ripple of discontent engulfs a land, are only a few individuals unable to concentrate on the repetitious claims of incriminating charm? (283)

To grasp the significance of that moment, a person must be immersed in the excellence of all goodness that can only be revealed in a futuristic revelation of finding peace through the acknowledgement of bizarre malformations. (284)

Why is dishonesty that is concealed in the agony of heightened despair, often hidden in a multitude of reproachable yet indecisive irregularities? (285)

Because the truest form of friendship is never spoken in anger but is only revealed when at least two persons forget the past that would never have been a reliable future. (286)

Will the unrelenting pursuit of revenge ever find fulfillment in the abstract cruelty of any contrite spirit that seeks a reward for finding a justification for vengeful enthusiasm? (287)

Only when obstacles in a life free from manipulative embarrassments solicit a needed response from any unyielding searcher of provocative merriment. (288)

Does an individual with a grateful heart ever take a reduction in payment that was not motivated by any advantageous interruptions? (289)

Understanding may change things that should not have been arranged by mere coincidence, but imperfections must never occur when payment is confronted by an abominable intermittent whimper. (290)

Why is the close proximity of any known question sometimes hidden in plain view by those who are least productive? (291)

Because the hollowness of a disappointment that brings unprofitable bewilderment to the structural integrity of meticulous hopelessness, is usually conceived in the gossip of unknown postulations. (292)

When is helpful advice an encouragement to those incapable of using a private conversation to conceal any disguised threat that has been verbalized for the sake of using too many vain compliments? (293)

When an individual who must always vacillate between deliberate skepticism and pure nonconformity considers an unreliable host as one who never learned the proper procedures for bridling a wayward tongue. (294)

Is it right that an advocate of saving the planets economical system strives for the perfection of a suppressed anger that will never be evaluated by the apathetic attitudes of someone who really cares? (295)

Not unless innuendos that are spoken in haste have determined that undeniable insinuations have become intoxicated by their own need to interrupt the informed enlightenment that strives to subdue the knowledge of a favorite relative. (296)

Can disappointment sometimes obstruct the need for a resolution that does not impede the justification of thwarted efforts? (297)

Only when suspicions abound in the sphere of pretentious obscurity that is often initiated by formidable dispositions that try to overshadow the rare shortcomings of invalidated motives. (298)

Why are the irrelevances of illogical thoughts of conjecture generally considered worthless when combined with the unskilled persistence of heartless acts of regrettable kindness? (299)

Because any individual who settles for the mediocrity of the moment will someday relinquish all rights to those who attempt to subjugate inconsistent beliefs in superficial impulsive character assassinations. (300)

Session 4

"The reasons for simulated speculations"

Why does the guarded enthusiasm of a few mischief-makers, infect all who attempt to pass through the moment of shameless fears? (301)

It is because irrefutable evidence of a suspected witness will often conjure up visions of anxious enthusiasm that need not be challenged by any mortal. (302)

Is nothing ever really gained by deliberate sarcastic restraint? (303)

Only things gained by deceitful disregard for profane pleasantries can ever spare any momentary funds for those who are in desperate need of complicating enduring relationships. (304)

Why is restlessness sometimes concealed among the mist of a fog that will not hide from anyone seeking to destroy the impervious impressions of flawed incompetence? (305)

It is because everybody who really cares about the feelings of simplistic individuals must always choose to divulge their fragile beliefs to others concerning the complexities of unthinkable disbeliefs. (306)

Does a boorish self-centered wanderer, who is often misguided by any new idea that proclaims knowledge gained by deceit, ever appreciate inconvenient wisdom? (307)

It is only appreciated by a wanderer who is patiently waiting on someone who is never on time and forgets to refrain from coughing when pressed for an immediate response to an unspoken answer. (308)

Will an individual who always looks for the absurdity behind blind ambitions someday find the need to question all interpretations that are not proved by scientific abnormalities? (309)

If they realize behind every lunatic is a person who cared not to be noticed by demented phobias. (310)

Can the disrespect of authority usually be traced back to a deficiency of leadership from an authoritarian figure that preferred to abandon the responsibilities of guiding a rebellious temperament that is continuously searching for the self-absorbing misunderstanding of naive disrespectful imaginations? (311)

Only when a person discovers that pondering less when attempting to ponder more will always lead to a road rarely found in the distance on a path that never intersects. (312)

When should a person never shake the hand of an individual who cannot explain the purpose behind the descriptive itemization of malicious spitefulness? (313)

When they come to understand that every penny saved will only add to the collection of accumulated change taken from those who spend what others will not share. (314)

Do motives that are never tested tend to test situations that are less likely to perform under the least desired alternatives? (315)

Not unless contentment that is predisposed to negotiate anger tends to regret the persistent outcomes of situations that never transpired in the first place. (316)

Why does lingering longer in the least desired moment often hinder the propulsion of lasting intentions that rarely reflect the sudden impact of impending prevailing silence? (317)

Because individuals who strive to live the life of foolishness continue to long for the fruitlessness that is conducive of a dream that only longs for the pursuit of the unlikeliest impossibilities. (318)

Will the equity that is impartial to absolute truth ever regret the extravagance found during the search for the truest form of generosity undisclosed by considerable considerations? (319)

Not unless the newness of all innovative inclinations is always preferred over the oppressive nature of an unresponsive countenance that succumbs to apathetic slothfulness. (320)

Should the pleasantness of prefect disillusionment ever be captured by the inspirational obligations of continuous freedoms vanquished by the misrepresentation of broad-minded tolerance? (321)

Yes, if the insufficient pettiness that survives the neglect of a sequence of events actually resides in the minds of those who must endure sequential meaninglessness. (322)

When are predetermined agendas inadequate for the assumed prognosis of undetermined confusion? (323)

They are only adequate when the entryway to any heartfelt sentiment is comprehended by the disingenuous pandering of a precocious isolationist. (324)

Can a smiling face be reflective of a happy heart that does not trivialize the reasons for laughter that does not exist? (325)

Yes, if the individuals forgetting to overlook any solicited opportunity for the obvious admiration of respective idolizations are never remembered in due time. (326)

Can the tedious introspection of any person accused of supporting the solitary cravings of lethargic abandonment, ever be understood by mere scrutiny of basic ideas? (327)

Only when others realize that taking a break can never become a substitute for a job well done in the mere confusion of an undisturbed momentary event. (328)

Do all people who breathe the pure air of unrestrained freshness, understand the unpretentious absurdity of the secret impurities that are hidden from all who admire the perplexities of unwanted bewilderment? (329)

Only if they believe that quiet times filled with moments of pleasant sounds and wishful thinking seldom blend into the landscape of latent diminished returns. (330)

Can demented brilliance that permeates the shades of color radiating from the untold stories of wanderers, ever travel on the majestic journey of alluring silliness? (331)

It can only travel on its journey when the melodious songs of freshness fill the air with rhythmical enchantments of invisible poetic brilliance. (332)

Why does nobility that ceases to fascinate all who observe the lavishness of its affluent exuberance, sometimes decay into a frenzy of infuriating contemplations that lack the deceit of any prolonged importance? (333)

Because never knowing what not to do is best left unnoticed by the confusion of make-believe information that has become disorientated by charitable uselessness. (334)

Why is always planning to plan a detrimental illusion that will seldom be filled with the foolishness of irrational mundane thoughts, captivated by unselfish jealousy? (335)

The reason for this is that the brilliant manifestation of the temporary sometimes replaces the desire to prepare others for the inevitable allurement of contrived pleasantries. (336)

How can the subjugation of comparative opinions make the profound assumption that pluralistic attitudes often circumvent the benign attitudes of the few? (337)

Because subdivided decadence is sometimes never appreciated by those who possess a finite knowledge of the wisdom of infinite comprehensible reality. (338)

Can the mass population that slumbers behind the most sacred imperfections, understand the magnitude by which temporarily structural attainment is aligned with the gravitational force of pivotal constructs? (339)

Only those individuals who try to control every aspect of obligatory grandeur can ever hope to be understood by anyone whom posses the narrow-minded views held by a few sentimental neophytes. (340)

Will the constant cultivation of circumstantial competence hide from anyone who demands an immediate verdict from an unquenchable desire for a vivid understanding of essential tangible competence? (341)

Not unless maximizing the message from a memorable moment leads to the sensational rationalization that people who do not think frequently, try to intellectualize the gloom of a pitiful humorous lament. (342)

Is picturesque indifference least attractive when spoken in the brevity of haste that is associated with the discords of unpleasantness? (343)

It is only least attractive when systematic negotiations of randomly selected conglomerations threaten the very wellness of beings that pursue the sublime gloom of stereotypical caricatures. (344)

Why does domesticated insignificance generally soften the hearts of those whose minds search for the illusion of a stranger without impetus? (345)

Because any change that initiates the suggestion that there must be an evolution in the frequency of supreme thought will in itself be doomed to the garbage heap of temporal obscurity. (346)

Is it true that a person who is misguided and mislead will likely misjudge the trickery of an individual filled with impulsive meekness? (347)

This is only true when that person believes that spontaneous ingenuity spoken with a sarcastic tonal inflection is an essential part in fulfilling the agenda of a populace that idealizes the perplexities of the renowned plausible advancement of self-denial. (348)

Why do some people believe mutual respectability to be a peculiar annoying trait that is sometimes exhibited in the lives of a dedicated few that forget the fundamental principles that should have been deposited in the despair of heighten boredom? (349)

Because they also believe that flamboyant fragmentation of questionable apportionments can be equally divided among the shareholders of frivolous fabrications. (350)

Do pulsating embellishments occasionally deify the explanations found in newly discovered authentic shallowness? (351)

Pulsating embellishments seldom defy the explanations, when those who assume to never know enough resent their constant complaining without compassion. (352)

Do unique talents that are squandered by those who seek the selfish desires of cynical skeptics, nervously anticipate the coming of a nearly perfectly proficient sentiment? (353)

They only nervously wait when they believe that confounding any situational confrontation can be accomplished by the misinterpretation of an acceptable argument gone berserk. (354)

Should someone always strive to improve the extensions of prosperity that forever reaps the furrows of inflated pride? (355)

An individual must always strive for excellence until they are confronted by a being that habitually lives to communicate the importance of liberating annoyances that are found sulking in a pool of tranquil criticism. (356)

When is gentleness the most sought after attribute by those who are captivated by the mundane chores of years that will always remain in the memories of forgetfulness? (357)

Any individual who is capable of recalling methodical anguish is able to encourage others to overlook the pertinence of forthcoming unnecessary modifications. (358)

Why do pleasant surprises warm the inner being of those individuals who never recognize a speck in the eye of those who behold the beauty of inward regret? (359)

The reason for this is that wise fools never appear foolish to individuals who do not seem to be effortlessly manipulated by a framework of inadequate deficiencies. (360)

Will careful examination of a factual manuscript lead to a more abrupt schism among acquaintances that thought they were not related? (361)

Only if those who think that they are crazy realize that they are most of the time only fooling the odd behavior of others who must constantly admonish the ignorance of warped behavioral insanity. (362)

Why do people who possess a contemptuous disdain for the finer things of life, often struggle to disapprove the desirable neglectful arrogance of those who always slander the dreamer in us all? (363)

It is because they have found that the greatest memories are those that are a continuation of tranquil thoughts manifested in the delicate feelings of a placid unassuming countenance. (364)

Can the illogical stupidity of an arrogant fool be sustained through the benevolence of an isolated pulsation from a frivolous debacle? (365)

Not unless questionable uncertainty is normally defended by flimsy excuses that elude even the best of fraudulent suggestions. (366)

How often does the lethargic framework of a progressive innuendo disappear in the darkened hall of pretentious injustice? (367)

When a person who is not an unobtrusive individual that is easily rewarded, overlooks superficial pettiness created by unsolicited compliments. (368)

To the person who does not perceive serenity, does the quiet hush of a secluded tempest frequently permeate the very essence of suspicious cynicism? (369)

Only when a solitary life is lived among the clamoring zeal of prudent individualism that often resolves nothing it its march to a path of admirable insolence. (370)

Can any spiteful person who must always try to explain away an insult ever be trusted to assume a position of authority that is essential for the well being of conquered poets? (371)

Not unless they can find an individual who seeks the rewards of happiness and becomes trapped in the realm of dullness that is never bored or rebuked by complacency. (372)

Is it a wise choice to inspire an outsider who is rarely predisposed to confuse the facts with truths that should never be scrutinized? (373)

It is only a wise choice when remarks spoken with a flare of dutiful conceit are sometimes given away as presents to those immersed in the flavor of virtue that lacks honesty. (374)

Will a person who never rebukes an individual for forgetting a special occasion, someday in return be rewarded for striving to pursue the senseless meaning behind any spectacular endeavor of conscious thought? (375)

Yes, if the person is unaffected by the simplicity of a mind that usually indulges in ominous situational circumstances that often resemble the tranquil moments of suspicious assurances. (376)

Why is chatter that proceeds from loose lips, like a smirk that is seldom betrayed by a slothful person filled with cunning egotistical respect? (377)

Because dependability is a highly sought after character trait that is often suppressed by an individual who chuckles at blunders that were unintended to cause panic in the streets of professional dualistic pluralism. (378)

Can the natural impulse of an animated individual be understood with occasional irregularity that centers on the unified purpose of positional attitudes? (379)

Only when impromptu meetings bring an insightful look into the mind of someone whom attempts to categorize the exceptionality of those individuals who admire silence with the same importance as they do humanitarian gatherings. (380)

Are the inert emotions of someone who is void of emotional apathy an unnatural trait of those who provoke the misery of motionless silence? (381)

Yes, and the fashionable decline in commonly displaced resentment is a perplexing thought for anyone who cares for unsolicited reason behind the immediate decline in the authorization of unbiased prejudice. (382)

Must inferiority complexes permanently remain in compliance with state regulations that have been organized for the best possible demise of creative thought geared towards future financial independence? (383)

Not unless a brief yet abrupt ending to a serve scolding can be appreciated by those who always refuse to replace lost values with an emerging freshness of older ideas. (384)

Why does the hostile irritability of a cantankerous soul usually find liberation from the argumentative consolations that focus on the nourishment of futile ideas? (385)

Because the newness of an ultimate control that seeks the prestige of unsolicited applause, will often hide itself among the crowed fragrances of assumed flattery. (386)

Is it always an insult to partially tease anyone who refuses to accept the gentle mockery of a kindhearted humiliating experience? (387)

Only when opinions that lead to unresolved arguments always seek to restore the convictions of those who posses the perplexing arrogance of never striving to be wrong when they are always right. (388)

Is it true that a person who seeks to care about assumptions that depend on the outcomes contained in the whole essence of life, will seldom be disappointed by those who determine to throw away the tattered remains of memories that were too presumptuous to be repeated? (389)

It is only true if they posses the abominable ability to predict the future tense of subjugated opinions that will have a devastating effect on the pulse of preexisting mannerisms. (390)

Is the hazardous nature of things yet to be determined, reflective of a conceptual need to replace the good with items that never appreciate the pure delight contained in superficial thoughts? (391)

They are only reflective when the best intentions of a fruitful life lived in disarray can be fully appreciated by a careless thought that contends for the notoriety of genuine recognition for a job well done. (392)

Why is the soothing calm among the tempest of confusion only awarded to those who find the fondness of the ordinary more practical than the adornment of unsubstantiated accolades? (393)

Because inevitable boredom continually permeates the life of unsuspecting strangers who visit a town in a county where no one cares about the feelings of a transplanted impostor. (394)

Is fulfilling the basic needs of fulfillment, a basic need known only to those who must attempt to find fault in the thoughts of the mundane and least respected? (395)

No, not unless the person who is well versed in the art of intuitive compromise is the one best equipped to receive the rewards from previous benefits that contained the highest standard of selective virtues. (396)

Will a spiteful heart that only lives to vindicate a scoundrel ever become a causality of the newest form of retrospective harassment? (397)

The possibility only exist if sympathetic flexibility that is indigenous to those achieving triumphal success, is never disregarded by anyone who listens to the voices of a sympathetic transgressor seeking purposeful intent. (398)

When is the upward spiral of a discernible perception paramount in the complete understanding of integrity that has become malignant in its quest to achieve the highest pinnacle of tasteless unethical integrity? (399)

When giving a little only to take a lot is never the best expression of a person who makes an attempt to verbally articulate the candid perspective of prospective crassness. (400)

Session 5

"Furthering the woeful tears of untamed boredom"

Why does the failure to whitewash a hoax encourage anyone who is filled with assumed neglect? (401)

Because humorous yet amusing jokes played upon someone who hides behind the security of a sophisticated gag, is often a puzzlement to the mind of a bystander who is trying in earnest to forget a disputed riddle. (402)

Will enthusiasm that lacks any sense of honor one day be relegated to the humiliation of disgraced impulsiveness? (403)

One day when divergent aptitudes reflect the need for enduring friendships to deny offensive peculiarities. (404)

Is the ability of others to discover culpability in the humor of artistic abnormalities, sometimes hastily proclaimed throughout the miserable excuses of those who never cared for sanctioned habits? (405)

Not unless a peculiar person is generally perceived to be null and void of any proficient indiscretions worth mentioning. (406)

Can originality that is egger to gain fame beckon to a previous time full of memories that dwelt on the primitive conjectures of flowering adulation? (407)

Yes it can, if a candid remark spoken in a harsh tone echoes in the halls of inflamed politeness that is yet to be birthed by inconsistency. (408)

Why does justifying a reason without even really seeking the truth behind a flagrant lie, lead only to the decline of genuine excusable permissiveness? (409)

Because temperance that lacks self-denial will one day grow into a liberated thought that couldn't be approved by those who respect vindication without the proper permission. (410)

Are preeminent concerns over an abundance of lavish abnormalities often inflamed by the condescending views of those who must always attempt to counsel the mind of anyone who hides from a superior intellect? (411)

This possibility exists only if a person who is always preoccupied with a sense of senseless perfection will permanently be bound to the truest form of forgetfulness that is least remembered. (412)

Does any response given in a time of grasping for a vision of abundant fulfillment leave an individual felling lethargic even at the height of desperation? (413)

Yes, if the individual understands that any associate who makes a humble attempt to accept the advice from a bitter rival will one day reap the rewards of unfamiliar circumstances that must be resolved by suitable sarcasm. (414)

Why are painful memories of past accomplishments never fulfilled by the hollow recognition of acquisitions acquired by deceitful initiatives? (415)

This is because to recognize a compliment when spoke in jest is an attribute worthy of a definitive answer given to any imaginary question. (416)

Will a person who must always impersonate the character of a well-known truism often cause an outbreak of energy that can never be contained by temporal materialism? (417)

Not unless a genuine compliment is only as sincere as the motive behind the actual grievance. (418)

Does adaptation without any regard to customs which have never been revealed, usually cause a person to seek the council of those who will never understand the genuine understanding of all that could be understood? (419)

Yes and it is always a challenge to reconcile without first modifying the certainty that lies beneath the befuddled absurdity of unknown fixed origins. (420)

Do flexible nuances abound in the realm of probability without any hope of complete restitution of supplemental compromise? (421)

They only abound when someone must confront a realistic person who loves the pluralistic continuance of dominating circumstances that must consider the unknown perplexities of undesired thoughtfulness. (422)

Will any person who seeks the admiration of those who search for the need to administer punishment to the unrehearsed ramblings of a sociopathic reprobate, one day find solace in the fact that others have often tried but never failed? (423)

They will only find solace when perseverance without solid evidence to back up the preference leads to a conflict of experience that has yet to be confronted by familiarity. (424)

Should an antagonist ever perform in front of anyone who lives a life full of conceit and sensibility? (425)

If the person is an advocate who stands up for the rights of others to proclaim the beauty of the natural and never attempts to graciously agree to meditate on the truths that can never be denied. (426)

Can an individual who is content to live a life full of distress, uphold the strongest convictions that prohibit the establishment of an alliance with a devotee of refined slothfulness? (427)

Any person who tries to live like a weasel and willfully wiggles without warning is only waiting to question whether or not a quarrel is essential when demonstrating the proper procedure for the avoidance of an impending dangerous situation. (428)

Can any known intruder who is lost from plain view ever intimidate an afterthought? (429)

Only when an individual who exaggerates an accomplishment that is without a blemish turns back to be exonerated by the same people who cry out in the bleak wilderness of constant wayward futility. (430)

Are anxious thoughts often preceded by an awareness of enthusiastic liveliness that is always dissatisfied with accusations that never have been proven? (431)

If disparaging words are construed with the same intent that can never be justified by intellectual animosity. (432)

Why is attentiveness that lacks awareness never acceptable to those who strive to form a bond between people who never doubt anything worth doubting? (433)

Because those who listen much only hear the words that others find offensive even to remember. (434)

Can the friendly confines of a broken promise live within the peaceful storm of a raging scheme? (435)

Yes, and hatred that is always directed toward the great void of common agreement will one day be revealed in the antiquated age of events that will never take place. (436)

Why will public demonstrations of an unexplained declaration soon be forgotten in the chaos that must be analyzed by a person whose mind shrinks in a brain too large? (437)

A person who opposes reason will one day find the meaning that changes not when confronted by the mere mention of annoyances embraced by docile charm. (438)

Should a proud heritage be a meager substitute for believing in an idea that has been activated by an incident that never occurred during a blue moon? (439)

Not unless a person who manipulates the apathetic indifference of a morbid pleasantry tries to act human without even trying. (440)

Why has the world always had a fascination with an individual who could recite eloquent ramblings that tickle the ears but not the intellect of persistent bore? (441)

Because the delectable delicacies of benign thoughts often taste like food that can never replace the purest flavor of an idea that has no substance. (442)

Is delegating authority the obvious solution needed to solve problems that should never have emerged from a contrite manifestation in a change of heart? (443)

Not until innocent suspicions yearn for ambitions mobilized by the irreverent disapproval of ostentatious spur of the moment insolence. (444)

Can speculative conjectures continuously confuse a person who attempts to postulate presumptions that slander the confederation of an individual who exhibits a misguided demeanor? (445)

Only to those who must always be warned of divided loyalties and never allowed visit the uppermost precipice of collaborations achieved by convenience. (446)

51

Why is materialist denigration always presumed to be a portion of a diabolical plan to unite the autonomous nature of permanently endorsed nonsense? (447)

Because unproductive fruitlessness is repeatedly ostracized by obstructions that refuse to admit their need to dominate every situation. (448)

Is basic justification ordinarily an attempt by those who posses a less attractive metabolism to dominate every conversion that is not centered on disgusting admonitions? (449)

Not unless foundational confusion displays prejudicial displeasure to any lament that does not recognize the achievement of someone who has not been approved for renouncing his or her lack of stupidity. (450)

Why do fatigued outdated afterthoughts seldom thrive in the cesspool of new ideas that have tried to envelop the desolate caustic lightheartedness of a riddle void of pretentiousness? (451)

It is probable because those who refuse to initiate a restructuring of forgotten dreams will be inevitability washed away by the mystical folly that refused to surrender to momentary monumental truths. (452)

Is speaking more when thinking less a dangerous path to travel if being observed by idiots who are not also smart? (453)

Yes, especially when pretentious behavior that is presumed to be boastful is only a pretense of a deeper flaw in character, which is usually hindered by deception. (454)

Why is it an enormous mistake to attempt to deceive a klutz that is always boastful to somebody who wanders in the path of an unrevealed nightmare? (455)

Because any person who attempts to counsel a clown will seldom see the light at the end of a tunnel that was never meant to exist. (456)

Will those who remain steadfast in the face of any known momentary illumination, always test a person who presumes to be wise? (457)

Not unless a pompous fanatic encourages others to escape from the realities of wishful thinking that suppresses every known probability of fleeting brevity. (458)

Can the shinning luster of dampened impertinence ever abound in the bureaucratic confusion of compelling thoughts? (459)

Only when a brawl that begins as a significant interesting squabble calms a cordial fight. (460)

Why is furthering a career without the knowledge of superficial displacements never a wise choice to make in a world deprived of endless elusiveness? (461)

Because trite sayings are never appreciated be those individuals who must always leave the consequences to somebody who yearns for an early diagnosis. (462)

Is a grateful heart ever deprived of contentment when an outpouring of consolation is not far-removed from the expectations of those who are prepared? (463)

It is deprived of comfort when a complete waste of time can view the precepts of notable exceptions. (464)

Do immeasurable days of endless praise await those who desire the admiration of those individuals who inhabit the land of simplistic mood swings? (465)

Not unless fools dream without comprehending that periodic dozing is a good thing. (466)

Will always trying to race with the wind usually leave those who strive for perfection without a true feeling of the purest form of fulfillment that is seldom denied? (467)

Only when they discover that by trying to lessen the disappointment by sharing the truth is the reason for hiding beneath the outer exterior of chosen dilemmas. (468)

Can a person endure fame without first seeking a proverbial negative response to an infrequent character mannerism that was not recognized by positive impulses? (469)

Yes, just as staying calm in any situation is seldom viewed as justification for venting an outpouring of neurotic embellishments. (470)

Why will striving for the cutting edge of perfection often lead to the destruction of positive negativism? (471)

The reason for this is that a person who is thought of as wise will usually disappoint those who are never impressed by the outward love of deprived inwardness. (472)

Will showing affection without displaying an attitude of nostalgic reflection confuse anyone who has determined in their own hearts that there is never any good in nothing? (473)

Not unless there is a complete understanding that intermittent substantial impulses are essential for all individuals who need the affirmation of subjugated values. (474)

Should perfecting problems of endlessness ever replace the knowledge of known replacements? (475)

Only if those that try to find the rubbish left behind by the knowledge of pleasant perfection will never search for lessons that should not be learned. (476)

Can regrets ever replace the prerequisite to state the hidden facts of fictionalized negativity? (477)

Not unless radical associations are welcomed by those who dictate the hidden invitations of uncontrolled lies. (478)

Why do recollections that are never loved, collapse when tempted by worrisome thoughts? (479)

This is because parasites usually flock to the aroma of success that should never have been anticipated. (480)

Do motives that are never tested tend to test situations that are less likely to perform best under the least desired alternatives? (481)

Only when happiness that is predisposed to negated anger tends to regret situations that never occurred at all. (482)

Will lingering longer than lasting intentions often risk the rewards of sudden silence? (483)

Only if a person realizes that becoming a jerk without forgetting to find the pursuit of happiness is usually impossible to determine without the need for practice that could never be achieved. (484)

Why do some peculiar individuals live in the land of abnormal where nothing seems to believe in predictability? (485)

They have come to an understanding that the subjugation of relative ideas makes the assumption that pluralistic attitudes circumvent plagiaristic tendencies of remorseful regression. (486)

Do those who pursue a finite knowledge of the wisdom that surrounds infinite comprehensible reality ever appreciate subdivided decadence? (487)

It is never appreciated unless somebody can find a home that has been left behind in the darkness of undisturbed preconceived hallucinations. (488)

Can unknown transferred differences often determine the result of shared unintentional connections? (489)

Yes it can, just as waiting for unfulfilled dreams often creates an aspect of nervousness that focuses on unnatural actualizations. (490)

Can sympathetic challenges change the attitudes of abandoned icons that are symbolic of emotional motifs? (491)

Not unless elemental metaphors that exist in the prehistoric misery of secret imperfections can be rehabilitated by antiquated old-fashioned objectiveness. (492)

Why is the past never present for very long? (493)

The reason for this is that it is a difficult challenge for any human being to listen to untold tales by individuals who are clueless of the need to expand on the past exaggerations of stories that could certainly not have ever been understood. (494)

Is it ordinarily easy to find an explanation to any problem that does not posses patterns to regret? (495)

No it is not easy, because a person who finds favor in the eyes of the beholder will never find happiness in the values of those who must escape from their own delusions of one-dimensional grandeur? (496)

Do parasites generally flock to the sweet smell of success that radiates from the individualist necessity for everyone to comprehend the purpose for a scent gone sour? (497)

They only flock when the need to know is seldom known by those who need to comprehend the vast nature of the reasoning behind systematic probabilities. (498)

Why are unexpected rewards occasionally a surprise to those expecting enthusiastic applause from everyone who sometimes ponders offensive encouragement? (499)

They are seldom a surprise because pompous pride is never observed by an individual who is always impressed by those who look for a cloudless day in the stillness of the night. (500)

Session 6

"Waiting for wasted dilemmas"

Should a person stay away from a dog that bites unless it flees from a flea that flutters? (501)

A person should only stay away if the individual believes that confidence regularly confounds anyone who will listen to the echoes of concise guarantees. (502)

Is nothing ever gained if the pursuit of unhappiness is obtained through the by-product of negative optimism? (503)

Nothing is ever gained unless others remember that forgone conclusions can only be achieved by pardoning the negligence of uneducated philosophies. (504)

Will creating a perception of knowing all things, produce a lifeless void that cannot be denied or avoided? (505)

Creating a perception of knowing all things is entirely based upon the belief that shortening of the day is a naive concept to those who believe in the uselessness of disavowed embarrassments. (506)

Why is an option of disappointment never an excuse for the positive reinforcement of simple contextual strategies? (507)

This is because problematic spontaneity is a characteristic only found in the character of an individual who displays a profound sense of suppressed shamelessness. (508)

Is it possible that mitigation handled in a manner that is shrouded in a false sense of disgraceful shame, will one day be rewarded with a decreased renewal of diminishing rewards? (509)

It is only possible if wanting more when needing less leads to an illegitimate state of awareness that is suppressed by a precipitous influx of euphemistic confessions. (510)

Can a person who generally disowns the feelings of another individual, wind up insulting their own need to seek the approval of an influential advocate who seeks the elimination of all competent peculiarities? (511)

Not unless it has been determined that an ignominious state of confusion is only infectious to a chosen few who live in a world that is detestable to domesticated hairless felines. (512)

When a society obliterates the need for sudden irregular curiosities, will only those elite few who detest competence at any level of proficiency approve practical self-denial? (513)

Not unless those who practice self-denial believe that if a flame is extinguished in the middle of an autumn night, it will wander in the land of smokeless aromas forever. (514)

Will primitive thoughts that become the norm, one day be remembered no more when the thoughtless ones roam the earth with packs of wingless worms? (515)

They will only be remembered when a depraved heart must always seek the compassion of those who flounder in a fluttering bouquet of enthusiastic anticipations. (516)

Can never knowing the need to know, always lead to nothing worth knowing? (517)

Yes, if a plentiful supply of needed empathy is always waiting for someone around the bend of immeasurable ridiculousness. (518)

Are the complexities of life by no means thought of with the same speculative conjecture that usually withdraws from the preposterous ramblings of rational afterthoughts? (519)

They are only thought of in this way because conceptual ideals sometimes originate from hypothetical complications that should never have been established by buffoons who thought they knew too much. (520)

Why do moderate insults abound in a chasm where right is never thought of with a conscientious heart and there is always someone attempting to summarize the intricate insanity which comes from only pursuing slanderous compliments? (521)

Because moderate insults are like a bottomless pit, where someone who misuses the slanderous language of deceit brings calm to any pleasant situation by speaking words in jest. (522)

Can offenses that malign the walls of intolerance frequently bring reproach to anyone who seeks the formalistic etiquette of a disquieted honeybee? (523)

No, because a wrong can never be complete if it was never erroneous in the first place. (524)

Will an abundant bounty of scholarly advice ever be appreciated by a society that is obsessed with the pursuit of finding the knowledge of truth, which abides only in the wasteland of nothingness? (525)

It can only be appreciated when a society believes that stupidity is always waiting to be displayed in a private public place, where individuals who claim to know everything about a subject that makes no sense at all strive for a feeling of glee without remorse. (526)

Is it true that in is never out when out is never found? (527)

Yes, because empty thoughts from a wounded mind will soon be forgotten by the unexpected insignificance of moments embraced by misfortune that is discreetly abandoned. (528)

When will intellectual prominence that always strives to please anything which is permissible, unintentionally resist the temptation to deceive anyone who consults conventionally unattainable understanding? (529)

When the watchful eye must never be allowed to randomly select the casual order of words that are believed to be authentic but only make sense to someone who does not exist. (530)

Why do silly songs of pure delight have no real value to anyone except to deliberately confuse someone whose ideas are embraced by irrational senility? (531)

A reason for this could be that those who seek the folly that has been hidden in plain sight will regret the day that truth was revealed from the mouth of a self-proclaimed genius that could not stop devouring the praises of a fool. (532)

Can a person who does not understand the understandings of knowing the knowledge of wise wisdom, often be confused by confusion that has not placed limits on limitations? (533)

Yes, if this individual believes that accommodating the honest accolades from an insincere conspirator will always be observed by those who confront guarded allegations that have been authorized by a master of habitual misfortunes. (534)

Why do random ideas that radiate from the top of a mountain often infect the minds of all who are possessed by a brain that has been infested by irresponsible insinuations? (535)

Because those minds have come to the realization that absolution often seeks the advice of those who grasps for straws without faces. (536)

How can associating with a friend who complains once a day, create a custom that only destiny could deny? (537)

Because a lethargic individual who properly adapts to the cultivation of any achievement, will never be exploited for the sheer pleasure of exploring the applicable misuse of prosperity diminished by lavish embellishments. (538)

Will the skillful cultivation of new ideas for the benefit of the wellbeing of others be doomed to failure, if honest nauseating probabilities are not tested by the spasmodic accusations of a casual confidant? (539)

This can only take place if ingenuity that accommodates the lack of satirical pity, digresses into a pathetic downward spiral that can only exist if sustained by certified condemnations. (540)

Why is recognizing an accolade that could have spoken meaningful utterances, an accomplishment that only a few valiant individuals have ever dared to accumulate? (541)

It is only a feat for those who continually rationalize the doomed exploits of a make believe complaint and seldom justify the ill-fated descriptions they so vaguely attempted to explain. (542)

Will a factual hypothesis lack a true sense of conformity whenever it is exposed to the trueness of everything that should never have been rebuked? (543)

It will lack a sense of conformity when culpable liability is doomed to success and left alone by those who generally associate longevity with sincere candor. (544)

Is a good reputation ever a substitute for an attempt by others to give a reason for resisting embracing the embarrassments of a materialistic philanthropist? (545)

No, because an explanation of old ideas often lacks the innovation of the antiquated results that will never be forgotten by anyone who forgets to forget. (546)

Do the ancient tales of tattletales live in the hearts and minds of those afflicted with a compassion that cannot be condemned? (547)

They sometimes live in a heart where the past is never present in the places least forgotten by the remembrance of everything that contains nothing. (548)

Does biding your time ever carry the same clout as bidding farewell to the habits of unrelated patterns? (549)

It only carries clout when those who tarry seldom carry within them a need to bury something that never existed before, except in a mind where thoughts once roamed wildly without any specific boundaries. (550)

When will a person who tries to conceal an encumbrance without first shackling its contents, be left with an emptiness that only silence can find? (551)

When a pet mole that lives in a hole could care less about its significance in a world in which it could have lived a blissful life but chose instead to walk the path of a shrew. (552)

Can movement without motion hinder the pastime of any activity that agitates an animated reformer of radical malcontents? (553)

It is only a hindrance when intimidation that is always stimulated by suitable appreciated scorn attempts to vigorously attain exploits that can throttle any course of scholarly study. (554)

Does intolerable praise that is heaped upon an individual full of humility generally heighten the intensity of lesser-known simulations that will accomplish nothing worth repeating? (555)

Heightened intensity will only take place when chronic fixations that are dependent on fanatical obsessions lose their power when confronted by a flourish of flustered precepts, which have been designed to intimidate the most powerful mediators of debauchery. (556)

Can love that is seldom cherished ever mature into an exquisite blossom full of the bouquet of a hope that lacks the resolution to accept the veneration of true anticipation? (557)

Maturity takes place when overwhelming pressure never assumes that anything is real unless it has been confronted by true inspiration that has been converted to new ideals by old ideas. (558)

Would only a foolish person search for a truism in the midst of docile bewilderment? (559)

No, unless they thought that the shortest way around a problem was never through the back door of contrived frustration. (560)

Will customs that are accustomed to compromise, always seek the acceptance of judgmental deviations that lack devotion to circumspect deliberations? (561)

They will only seek acceptance when tears spring forth from a well that will only run dry if left undisturbed by a stream that trickles from a creek that will never become a river that flows into an ocean. (562)

Will a person who is sorry about nothing, find it almost impossible to overlook an apology that was fashioned by somebody who wasn't unquestionably regretful about the unimportant things in someone else's life? (563)

They will only regret apologies when someone suggests to them that an overloaded brain can never find rest from the abundance of new ideas that promise prosperity but without the need to redistribute the wealth of the knowledge of affluence that will never be attained. (564)

When will a behavior that is not intentionally modified, achieve the same stature of a blade of frost bitten grass that lives in a world where dirt is a king and sand is nowhere to be found? (565)

When undesirable consequences are created by ill-advised results that constantly try to provoke the anger of a person who suffers from an illness brought on by genuine patience. (566)

Is it ever possible for a boisterous prudent individual to sensibly enjoy watching just for a mere moment of majestic beauty, an adorable raccoon consuming leftover cat food? (567)

This is only possible when memories of distant undefined feelings torment the very nature of an unresponsive essence that often is detached from the reality of suggestive pretense. (568)

Who ever decided that the probability of an apprehensive mortal becoming a credit to a dying society that has become blinded by the graciousness of untested tenderness is about the same as a skunk trying to meow like a dog that thinks it is a tomcat? (569)

Those wise individuals who always believe that unexplained good-natured attitudes continuously confuse the present with a future that has no confidence in the past. (570)

Will trying to accomplish something without first possessing a willingness to become someone of importance, devastate anyone who yearns for a passion that can seldom be contained in an enthusiastic whimper? (571)

Yes, when articulated verbalizations that are uttered with candid frankness often display a distinctiveness that will always be endorsed by a self-proclaimed chosen few who lack the fortitude to even become unsuccessful in anything that is not attainable. (572)

Are clouds that slumber on the top of a mountain the only ones that can attempt to comprehend the deepest thoughts of the rain that resides within them? (573)

No, because staying focused on the job at hand is a challenging assignment for an individual who is fluent in every language that has not yet been discovered. (574)

Does a flea or a tic that is resting on a stick give much thought to the thickness of the fur where someday soon it will be hiding? (575)

The answer to this question is yes, because they also believe that the stupidity of a ladybug is usually an envied trait that is highly prized and sought after by those who consider themselves to be wiser than the minorities who will one day run rampant throughout the thoroughfares of unrestrained arrogance. (576)

Why is just one more time never enough for those who have relinquished the rights of their minds to the reigns of their dispositions? (577)

It is never enough because just doing anything for the sake of doing something should never become the sole reason for attempting to solve a problem before it has been prepared in retrospect. (578)

Why does the weariness for the concerns of objections that will never be determined, usually change nothing but the nature of the origins of feelings yet to be resolved? (579)

It usually changes nothing because educated proposals carelessly presume that certain outcomes are predetermined by out of town family members who devour too much food when sitting down to eat brunch. (580)

Is paying attention while somebody is thinking the only sensible ways to forget contemplations that were never remembered? (581)

Maybe, if someone accepts the fact that to understand a question before it is asked, a person must reject the impulse to speak from the knowledge that was once held captive in a mind where wisdom has become lost. (582)

Is it a true statement that a person is needed most when their needs are of utmost importance to the lives of the one which others in need seek encouragement? (583)

The statement might be true if those individuals who disregard intentional misrepresentation truthfully respect the limitations of allotted functions that must not be acknowledged. (584)

Do essential inspirational messages that are designed to confuse critical criticisms, often generate request that cannot be ignored? (585)

They can only be ignored when accuracy that is distorted by excellence refuses to consider looking for encouragement behind rocks that do not shed tears. (586)

Is giving less ever an option for giving more? (587)

Giving less is only an option when a fading dream that lingers near the precipices of oblivion, never finds the door that leads back to the threshold of insanity. (588)

Should a shadow always beware of darkness that lurks behind the limelight of daytime illusions? (589)

No, because keeping something straight is always difficult for a human who lives a life of running away from political recklessness. (590)

How long will progress that seeks the approval of those who hide from the rewards of unrewarded obedience wander in a void of emptiness that attempts to establish a village of unknown origins? (591)

Progress will only wander as long as basking in the dimness of a failure not yet realized causes perpetrators to wallow in the slime of underserved fellowship that is preoccupied with disappointment that has not been prescribed. (592)

Why do trustworthy well-balanced intentions sometimes arrive at a destination that has been chartered for them by the pretenders of gloom that are doomed? (593)

It is because a child does not show up on time to a spur of the moment mandatory event and the parent must attempt to check the pulse of those who never pause to remember the deeds of someone who lives a life patterned after the values of neurotic completeness. (594)

Do those who hide from a hidden agendum generally keep others that they love from devouring green apples that have no seeds? (595)

Not unless they believe that finding the reason for the true joy of all happiness should be the only reason a person would everyday scan the skyline for a goose that is trying to fly south with hummingbirds for the twilight of winter. (596)

Is it true that a person should never dwell on the willful dependence of irrational irritability or the outcome could cause a major conflict in a nation whose people know only how to sing but not speak? (597)

Yes, because a person should always be on guard against flattering words spoken with a latent intent that solicits a need in others to reflect on the main idea of a meaningless statement not yet birthed by a warped mind bent on enlightenment. (598)

Does the pressure of the moment mean nothing when compared to the mediocrity of all know rebuttals? (599)

It means only nothing if any perfect moment in time is destroyed by the individual who posses the finite capabilities of realizing that all is not as it should be, if only could be, would ever prevail. (600)

Session 7

"The folly of silliness revealed"

Are peculiar qualities often shared within the silence of babbling nonsense? (601)

Peculiar qualities are only shared when others believe that trying to confuse an uptight person who has never relaxed, may create an ultra confusing situations that might make it impossible to negotiate a split decision that could create dilutions of symbolic significance. (602)

Must constructive alternative views of derogatory simplistic attitudes always be encouraged in order for an intensification of optimistic deceitful perceptions to overrun the earth with all sorts of mysterious behaviors? (603)

Only encouraging descriptions worth mentioning must be expressed in a straightforward unsophisticated voice that does not communicate any sentiment other than to celebrate the commitment of dependability that cannot be pinpointed. (604)

Does endeavoring to struggle against all known individualist implications, motivate people who are trying to mend relationships that franticly seek to distance themselves from the impending defeat of perplexing mysteries? (605)

The only ones who are inspired are those who believe that any paradox that attempts to align itself with cynical existentialism will accomplish nothing but to accumulate an inordinate amount of uniquely designed philosophical questions. (606)

Why is it almost unbelievable beyond comprehension that an individual can bask in the light of a candle that will not burn? (607)

It is fundamentally unbelievable because trying to avoid acute boredom is a difficult habit to overcome if the symptoms are not apportioned in an appropriate manner that is not vulnerable to pessimistic promises. (608)

Why do some advocates for the policies of restraint often compromise at the initial suggestion of obstinate revelations that have begun to decompose? (609)

Advocates often compromise because they have determined that meaningless words sometimes when least expected tickle the intellect of those whose ears are usually closed to the harmonization of pleasant triteness. (610)

Why is a person who is always asking what time it is, usually oblivious to the natural order of all things that have been banished from unadorned isolationism? (611)

Any individual who thinks they have common sense but refuses to blink when another acquaintance nods, will never obtain the hindsight that is so essential in the handling of noxious limitations that have never been personal. (612)

Why do empty promises spoken with shallow candor often become a hindrance to anyone who smirks at raindrops that fall on the head of a rooster without ears? (613)

They become a hindrance because the lack of encouraging remarks that do not originate from a trustworthy source, often confuse those whose twisted minds can only comprehend the euphemistic clamor of pots and pans that have no handles. (614)

Will appealing charm that is obtained by the deceitful beauty of alluring ears benefit anyone except the person who is always waiting for silence in a room filled with invisible charm of latent adoration? (615)

The only benefit is to those who believe that if anticipation promotes an elevated state of nervousness it can only be observed in an individual's life when an innuendo is enlightened by camouflaged disappointments. (616)

Is it sometimes a unique challenge for person who is shy to express the joy of memories not forgotten by a friend of a distant cousin whose aunt was the brother of his sister's uncle? (617)

It is really not a challenge because negligent neglect often has no regard for the absolute disdain of genuine ancestral inattentiveness. (618)

Why do flippant attitudes never achieve the heights known only to those that ascend to the darkest heights of intellectual socialization? (619)

They never achieve intellectual socialization because an individual who craves the fulfillment of significant ignorance will only find significance in the admiration of an ultimatum, which will ultimately diffuse any unlikely situation. (620)

Why is it that generally a person whose cognitive perception is enhanced by the imaginative delights cannot be honestly encouraged by the transformation of meditative temperaments? (621)

It is difficult for the person to be inspired because the individual believes that the greatest contribution a person can make to a make-believe cause is to remain faithful to those who have lost their possessive competence. (622)

Can only a doomed destiny ever really understand the need to overcome the compelling perception of the artificial awesomeness of transferred tranquility? (623)

No, unless significant contentment surrounded by the lies of unprotected truthfulness is exasperated by the humiliation that surrounds the harmonious nature of fabrications spoken with a tone of sensitive sarcastic perfectionism. (624)

Is it possible for the loneliness of a clown to never be hidden from the laughter of the crowd who seeks to understand the hidden meaning behind the heartfelt cries of the emotionless perfectionist? (625)

It will always be hidden until the meaningful imaginative imagery of a perfectionist who is motivated by intuitive desire to withdraw from non-threatening anxieties, enables a person to discover contentment in the consciousness of a fragile psyche that mulls over interpersonal resolved conflicts. (626)

Do those who are always looking for the freshness of new ideas that will never satisfy their stupidity, mostly think of the shrewd thoughts from a wise council as out-of-date foolishness? (627)

Yes, because they try to share personal hurt and pain with those who have a difficult time admitting their authentic arrogance and believe it is also a major challenge even for those who feel secure when they embrace their own self-sufficiency to always complain. (628)

Are problematic circumstances that bring humiliation seldom resolved by an undeveloped hollowness that cannot be manipulated by an uncontrollable tongue? (629)

They are seldom resolved without the complete understanding that the resolution of predetermined tension can never be restitution for materialistic depravity. (630)

Why does the deceptive nature of a depraved countenance often confuse the steadfast convictions of anyone who places their complete trust in insecurities that lack a conscience? (631)

One reason for the confusion might be that highly esteemed individuals who are able to affectionately unveil their thoughts to others concerning the exquisite beauty of arrogant ignorance, will never be satisfied reflecting on carefully constructed laments that are void of any symmetrical awareness. (632)

Will a virtuoso whose only purpose in life is to dazzle others with a skillful flare that is only displayed by orangutans, one day in the future find out that fame is a temporary flame birthed by the byproduct of alter ego that only presumes to be intolerant? (633)

The virtuoso will only find out that popular insights into unpopular decisions will usually help stabilize the cause and effect of diminished helplessness upon cultivated hopelessness. (634)

Are rewards ever bestowed upon a creature that will always surrender to the erosion of ethical delusions that have been propelled into motion by a three-year-old unethical contract? (635)

Rewards are only bestowed on humans who make the choice to follow the road least taken that leads to the condemnation of an individual that has become disoriented and betrayed by comprehensible statements that are completely disconnected from a menagerie of affluent instantaneous perspectives. (636)

Does the desired result of candid appraisal genuinely matter to an individual who never was a real person in the first place? (637)

It matters only to an ambivalent person who possesses the intellectual sense of a dead zombie and often consumes the flattery of a piece of hard candy that was thought to be a jellybean. (638)

Is it frequently a major challenge for a bashful person to withstand the temptation to criticize warranted condemnation that has been cultivated by the scandalous intrigues of groveling admiration? (639)

It is a challenge if they have not discovered that the secret of effective artistry that fears the failure of rejection can be found in the solemn introductions of those who search for misfortune far from unfamiliar worthlessness. (640)

Do demented indulgences ever cater to the warmhearted deception that sometimes overwhelms the whimsical uneasiness of those that are not easily intimidated? (641)

Yes, they can be a hindrance depending on whether or only not illogical controversial eloquence is a curse to any blockhead whose tasteless cravings are restrained by a compelling genuineness to accommodate unemotional exaggerations. (642)

Do disparaging words remain steadfast when confronted by obstacles that struggle to repudiate unproductive ridicule? (643)

Disparaging words can only remain steadfast when idealistic objectivity is the unseen catalyst that occasionally aggravates the dogmatic emotional response from any individual who lacks the judgmental charisma of a centipede. (644)

Why must a prudent individual never divulge the hidden secrets of the "shameless ones" to anyone who celebrates the birth of every emotionless antagonist? (645)

Because prudent individuals accept the premise that the impulsive explosiveness of laughter may one day conquer a world that does not respond to riddles without expectations. (646)

Should a person who must always use profanity to describe any overwhelming situation not speak unless spoken to by an individual who is not a mother of someone's other brother? (647)

This person will not be able to speak with anyone because emotions that get in the way of longstanding goals should never have been allowed to sneak their way into the back door of any demented folly. (648)

Will vitamins taken daily with powdered water instead of milkless powder be exempt from the subsequent visitation of dissolved nutrients that could have never become minerals? (649)

They will never be exempt because frivolous falsehoods are the motto of any opponent who is making every effort not to become an adversary who is also known by all as a grower of rotten green tomatoes. (650)

Should lifelong determination ever be an acceptable prerequisite for determining the desired outcome of any competition that is not based on computational formula yet to be discovered? (651)

Only when the core desires of a genuine heartfelt expression need not ever back away from the worthiness of a starling unexpected revelation. 652)

Will misleading answers to misleading questions usually mislead a gullible person who was once misguided by a friend's miscalculated compassion? (653)

Yes, because only an unassuming blunderer that lacks the knowledge of a bug would ever make the assumption that broken glass bears no shame. (654)

Are words that do not serve a purpose, sometimes left abandoned by the will of those whose only goal in life is to eat a hamburger in the shade of life? (655)

They are sometimes left abandoned because the value of an autographed memento is only known by a selected chosen few who have taken it upon themselves to rationalize the limitations of artificial sensationalism that will never be comprehended by anyone not living in a country that does not yet exist. (656)

Will the constant pounding of drums by exuberant teenagers in a small crowed room drive a music teacher to drink cactus juice while fleeing to a place where the only sounds that can be heard are the fluttering of invisible butterfly wings? (657)

Not unless obnoxious attitudes presumed to be charming by all whose irresponsible actions have never absolved the childish behavior of youthful foolishness, hinders the advancement of deluded voracious phobias found only in the sand on a beach. (658)

Can a lazy person who hesitations are short lived, ever be promoted to a position in which the lost art of telling time is the responsibility of someone else? (659)

The lazy person can only be promoted when induced motivation usually last as long as it takes a tick to escape from the leg of a stray brown dog onto the back of a wild black and white cat. (660)

Is it wise to always remember to stay away from tiny little dogs that look like they're going to bite, unless they flee from giant moths that fly recklessly in the sky at night? (661)

It is wise, because inattentive preoccupations with invalidated compliments often cause a disproportionate disorganized episode that stimulates the outrage of dormant motionlessness. (662)

When is objective truthfulness a valuable treasure to all who anticipate misgivings that encourage the procurement of beneficial noxious delicacies? (663)

When an effervescent personality is often misunderstood as a gas that could not escape from the confines of a natural unobstructed structure and presumes to be guilty unless proven innocent. (664)

Does the methodical amicable influence of an affluent individual often deteriorate during a sudden misuse of momentary wasted time that was never valued by a contemporary culture? (665)

When nightmares never again abound in the pure light of darkness hidden beneath the glimmer of the gentle sunshine of a cloudless night. (666)

Do rebuttals that always rebuke others tend to reinvigorate the negative side of those who never say something positive about anything that could never be recognized as a derogatory statement? (667)

Rebuttals only reinvigorate an effective leader that refuses to reflect on past suggestions that were not initiated by a brain that could resist simultaneous changes at the spur of a moment. (668)

How do differentiated ideas expect procedures to be followed by the book, when they possess no covers and contain no words that are visible to eyes that are open to old concepts? (669)

Procedures cannot be followed because pre-approved provisions need less support when left alone to battle the competency that others have so futilely assessed. (670)

Will someone who has common insight into the hidden realm of tiny spaces generally find that those who wait at the end of a tunnel will never be invited to a party hosted by ill-humored comedians? (671)

Yes, because they believe that maximizing the gifts and talents of those who have no weaknesses are impossible tasks unless someone first stands up for the rights of all donuts who have lost their holes. (672)

Is it always essential that people who really think that they are humans keep their minds focused on the main goal of finding the purpose for the principles behind the differentiated frequencies of all things? (673)

Yes, because a person who has never been diagnosed as being almost sick will understand the importance of congenial wellness that really keeps us apart for any specific duration. (674)

Why do important interpretations usually strengthen the bonds between those who seldom generate interesting comments and those who interact with illustrative illusions? (675)

Sometimes basic questions trigger commonplace memories that often project a false sense of frustration to those who grumble about the outcome of elaborate privileges. (676)

Will control that cannot be accounted for seek to destroy the temporary social skills of those who do not posses any knowledge of multicultural essence? (677)

No, because so-called reflective memories sometimes limit the body's natural ability to produce the exact amount of adrenaline needed to evoke a smile when a chuckle has been abandoned. (678)

Will the monotonous moans of a monotone that seeks to embrace the uncharted world of karaoke create an unforgettable moment that will instantly sooth and comfort the ears of creatures who wish they could not hear anything? (679)

An unforgettable moment will be created because compromising quality for the sake of limiting literal interpretations will in the end create more problems then could have been foreseen by those who always attempt to control the disorder called laziness. (680)

Will following a road of bricks that have been painted yellow always lead to a dead end path where a legendary people live who once believed in the erroneous concept of probable nothingness? (681)

No, it will not lead to a dead end path because challenging stipulations that disregard solutions continuously intimidates the integrity of an inner peace where character hides and mediocrity dances to the melodies of forgotten traditions. (682)

Why do some people strive for superficial contempt when allusions await all who resist the disappointments that attempt to thwart the madness of fragile heartlessness? (683)

The reason for this is that those who demand something will one day have everything that nothing can buy. (684)

Can a stable foundation that is not secure ultimately test the purpose of despair that is contained in the restlessness of discouragement that is found in the relative standard of truth? (685)

It will only test individuals who try to give directions to others without first knowing that where they are might cause measurable panic within the inner circle of complete chaotic confusion. (686)

Why is the genuineness of that which is tangible and real in the present tense, only acknowledged by those who do not understand how to care for the past? (687)

Only individuals who constantly endeavor to find the best in someone, express a desire for temporal possessions that were bought and paid for by the dirt and grime of persons who follow the path of resistance least anticipated. (688)

Why do many individuals who want to become champions, proudly stand on the platform of unidentified perspectives that have become jaded by living on a planet that is occupied by a multitude of deceptions? (689)

Because any glutton who lives for the punishment of living a life void of knowing the friendship of loneliness, will one day regret telling anecdotes about enigmas that could not be comprehended. (690)

Will embracing the darkness in the light of day often turn a heart towards a mind that only dwells on the weakness of those who love to eat chocolate cheese cake during the last days of the months that point to an autumn sunset? (691)

It will only turn the hearts of people who are suspicious of a visitor who cries without ever laughing at hypocrites who shed tears without ever cracking a smile. (692)

Is it true that a finicky person who thinks too much and less than often, may one day find a thought or two that entered their mind and no longer resides in the same local or location? (693)

No, because some people who look for the answers of life in glass of water that is only half-full will sadly one day realize that they didn't even notice that there wasn't a glass at all. (694)

Why does making a list of things to do, not make any sense to anyone, if the only purpose for the list was to impress those individuals who solicit confusion through the exhaled breathes that they take? (695)

It doesn't matter how many times a person asks for a question unless somebody already knew the question before a complete description of the answer was made and it was all a waste of time. (696)

Why is it true that nothing is ever gained from something that never was intended to become the sole purpose for gaining anything? (697)

It is true that whoever usually makes the first move is normally the second person to realize that making the first move really was not as important as the first person. (698)

Will any individual who tries to make someone else happy, grieve over the day when laughter was confined to a life of silliness and inadvertent chuckles? (699)

Yes, since trying to separate the mind from specific thoughts is a daunting task that can only be accomplished when a misguided individual seeks to inspire their own greatness. (700)

Session 8

"Learning to say what nobody means"

Should the trepidation of unpopular common denominators equalize all uncommon visualizations? (701)

Only for people who take the time to stand on the edge of a forest waiting patiently to hear a songbird sing their name before they run into the woods to chase invisible unicorns. (702)

Can a textured personality whose frailty is hindered by uninhibited cleverness, become defensive when threatened by a competition that contrasts the stark reality of reasoning with that of persistent significance? (703)

It will only become defensive when discouragement that is full of rejection seeks to bring contentment into a life that feeds on the isolation of anguish and affliction. (704)

Will a person who is always facing a challenge often display the symptoms of exhilaration that are usually displayed during an episode of personal contentment? (705)

This individual will not only display the symptoms of exhilaration but also experience many woes while striving to seek that which was sought after before a sense of personal freedom clouded the minds of those who refute council. (706)

Is it possible for someone who is creative to feel both the pain of rejection and the euphoria of the disingenuous expressions of inward thoughts that will never find an insignificant glimpse of autonomous motivations? (707)

Yes, because finding the bottom line is a problematic task for a person to undertake if it is undertaken without showing any signs of drowsiness that is customarily associated with extreme alienation. (708)

Will an individual who contemplates the motivation for despair, ever experience the excitement that is generated by the influence of debilitating interactions upon a pivotal moment that has been trampled on by unworthy foolishness? (709)

Not unless the longevity of real life compulsions does not possess genuine emotions that are typically cut short by apprehensive concerns over anticipated nervousness. (710)

Do others whose lack of subjectivity is unable to process advanced concepts of generalized homogeneous conclusions, frequently disregard the necessity for locating the variation of objective ideas? (711)

No, because the visual recognition of understandable objections is usually noticed by persons who are representatives of a new age of reasoning that places the common sense of an intelligent dingbat in the honor of utmost esteem. (712)

Why is synthesized effectiveness often used by self-proclaimed keepers of the wisdom of perceived knowledge to shake the minds of those who really understand what is really going on in an authentic world that others seldom care to see? (713)

Because consistency that is continuously constant should never be wasted on the important things that demand a dependence on frivolous commonplace treasures. (714)

Is it always a challenge to offer advice to others that will one day be appreciated as much as a bronze token used at a tollbooth to pay for a toll road to nowhere? (715)

It is always a challenge because improvised sensitivity that lacks a false sense of personal internal frustration will usually lack the courage to challenge the catastrophic attitudes of individuals who lack the mental firmness and courage to stand up against the aftermath of unintelligible level headiness. (716)

Why does an intelligent individual who never presumed to be happy radiate a memorable aroma that might be diametrically productive to the emotional pulsations of counterfeit inspirational expressiveness? (717)

Is it because those who seek genuine wisdom will also pursue the significant proportions of genuine unconditional persistence? (718)

Do those that desire above everything else the beauty, wealth, and status that are associated with no strings attached, only love the rejection of failure. (719)

No, because a wise individual usually discovers that a person who values freedom will always experience every day the exhilaration of knowing that chasing happiness will only lead to having to leave behind the memories of humorous feelings. (720)

Why is the influence of an influential person only as charming as it relates to the self-aggrandizement of their self-serving pride? (721)

It is only as charming as genuine inattentiveness observed from a distance and is usually a sign so that the transcendent nature of absolute relationships will unfortunately one day disappear only to once again emerge as a superficial polecat. (722)

Does a person who thinks that they are kind but never says thank you usually care about every drop of rain that falls on dirt that is already wet? (723)

Yes, because an individual who always utters the phrase "I'm only human" is normally able to spot an alien walking down a crowded street wearing a swimsuit and smoking a humongous Cuban cigar that was secretly made in China. (724)

Why do people who usually invent elaborate schemes, only reside in the dreams of consciousness that each day proudly illuminates the sky at high noon? (725)

Because people who must engage in the fun filled activity of full-fledged disobedience, are often guilty of jumping to simplified juvenile conclusions that would otherwise go unnoticed by those who are not use to giving verbal assent to non-life threatening relationships. (726)

Why are middle thoughts the best thoughts for keeping the first thoughts from not finding out about the other thoughts that were never secret to begin with? (727)

Because some individuals believe that certain plastic egos sometimes ascend from the deepest pit of self-deluded rudeness and often cloak themselves in predetermined arrogance. (728)

Is it wise to not ask for a question unless you do not want an answer to the question that was taken from your answer? (729)

It is only a wise choice to not ask for questions by those who think they are better than others and who best spend their vanity time completing their self-centered pompous résumé in order to impress a wild pack of conceited wharf rats. (730)

Should a smart mouth with a rebellious attitude ever be allowed to speak one word in the presence of an authentic certified human being who can only be located when trying not to be found? (731)

Only when unambiguous yet unspecified rationalizations acknowledge that whenever an individual is brutally honest, undeserved compassion will never become preoccupied with insolent blatant goodness. (732)

Will the dawn of a new day that beckons all to sing a new song about the greatness of our imaginations and creative conceit, echo throughout the ages in the toilet thrones of our decayed foolishness? (733)

Not unless always knocking on an old metal door that does not exist causes colleagues who were just visiting to seek humiliation from other imaginary sources. (734)

Should a slippery sly slithering snake that is owned by an plague-ridden infidel, ever cross paths in the middle of a hot summer day with an out of it's mind gopher turtle that is slowly walking away from a broken relationship after being kicked out of its cherished abode in the earth? (735)

Yes, as incredible as it might sound and whoever has been accused of observing the creative energy of a spittle bug will one day soon be forced to accept the passionate pleas of mundane moments that usually wrestle with the meaning of a half-baked half-life. (736)

Should a once caring, considerate and compassionate person who has lost the desire to pet a cute domesticated little kitten, be properly rehabilitated by being licked in a public forum for forty-five minutes in the face by the slobbering tongues of half a dozen Giant Schnauzers whose best friends are skunks? (737)

Yes, when nothing seems to be going right and the best thing to do is to seek out the positive passive indifference of those who find comfort on a teeter-totter with no one to totter with. (738)

Will proclaiming your intent before ever determining your intended emphasis cause only heartache in the long run to those who have been deeply shaken by a deep sense of urgency to pass on to the next generation the life changing story about "the flea that knew too much." (739)

No because the best time for a person to sleep is when subdued silence is present during the time of day when rest is found not far from the quiet state of peacefulness where tranquility roams without fear of a loss of freedom. (740)

Why is the best part of the day the time of day that is set apart for the retrospective personal awareness of the reflection of a past job almost completed when very nearly done? (741)

Because the best part of the day is when an individual has acquired the knowledge of objectivity and has come to realize that subjective involvement is an even poorer substitute for tolerable enthusiasm that searches for happiness in the habitual acts of unappreciative kindness. (742)

Will people who slumber without ever sleeping, wander in a continuous torpid state of sluggishness until awakened from a deep sleep that is known only to them? (743)

Only as long as unrelated uncomplicated confusion is observed in the lives of those who never understand the conceivability of that which cannot be conceived. (744)

Why does a fish that swims in a small pond without water soon come to realize that maybe it would have been better to be a frog? (745)

It comes to realize that the secret to preserving the restored meaning of true success lies in the understanding of what is hidden within the forethought of the knowledge of the wisdom of lasting solutions that are always surrounded by tactful insights. (746)

Does coming to grips with a problem before the problem manifests itself into a dilemma ever steal maturity from the one who complains every time something good happens in their life? (747)

It takes maturity only when gas that will not pass inhibits the judgments and prudent counsel of those who never ingest a mild laxative without first taking a suppository. (748)

Why should material prosperity become a meaningless goal for those who squander their ability to express their disfavor with all whose impeccable credentials have been overlooked by individuals who live in a land of desolation? (749)

It should become a meaningless goal because a lofty obsession that creates a self-imposed satisfaction will become an obsession to all who attempt to confess that they often strive for the affirmation of covert unrelenting determination. (750)

Is silly funniness sometimes funnier when found in a place where funny silliness will not enter? (751)

It is only funnier when others realize that to continue to neglect something that has always been neglected is far worse than hiding from the fear of neglect itself. (752)

Should a person who must always be reminded to remember the less important things that should not have ever been forgotten in the first place, ever be allowed to be placed in a position where the fate of all mankind rest upon a small depleted deposit from the brain of an absentminded intellectual that is impossible to locate? (753)

Only when the person fails to find a purpose for the reason for pursuing why something has not yet been found, then and only then should a meeting be called to find out if what was worth finding was first reasoned through thoroughly and then finally forgotten. (754)

Why is reacting to how others react to any reactions very confusing to all who are easily confused by confusion? (755)

It is perplexing because those things that appear to be simple can only simplify the simplistic simplicity of the simplest things. (756)

Why is a sarcastic deceitful smile that lives on a face that usually frowns, known by all who seek the praises of someone who is only as great as their vain reflection in an inexpensive bathroom mirror? (757)

It is only known because insecurity that is displayed by a person of youth during a very intense disrespectful verbal exchange, is reminiscent of what the contents looks like when a stomach while digesting dinner has thrown out of its mouth spaghetti with a large vegetable salad. (758)

Are slanderous individuals who constantly complain about everything, often bitter about past complex malicious schemes that they were unable to tolerate while hiding underneath the grumblings of a flourish of venomous compliments? (759)

They are often bitter because spontaneous recommended weaknesses are only appropriate for diagnosing the fundamentals of familiar principals not yet revealed. (760)

Is a theoretical understanding of selected techniques only made possible by the rarest of opportunities that demonstrate the ability of someone to develop a selective sense of methodology that has been determined to be useless in indicating suitable hourly progress? (761)

It is only made possible when others come to the understanding that expressiveness is an outward manifestation of the feelings that are critically necessary for the understanding of the development of the thinking process that is an essential component needed in order to understand theoretical mumbo-jumbo. (762)

Why is the necessity of significant relationships in the continuation of the establishment of progressive significant occurrences, a fundamental prerequisite needed to gain unique worthless awareness of undesired comprehension? (763)

It is a prerequisite because self-observation is a highly regarded technique used by the extinct Siberian monkey to decode the imprint of reactive interactions on the minimization of counterproductive ideas. (764)

Can those who sometimes comprehend the deceitful articulations of a depraved mind that embraces the use of profound useless rhetoric, cherish only interactive significance? (765)

Not unless qualified characteristics that are occasionally displayed by those who always resist opportunities to access whimsical capricious celebrations, manage to eloquently articulate the practical peculiarities of premature impatience. (766)

If extremists usually react first to differing views, can they maintain a balance between concrete deception and provocative elitism? (767)

They can only maintain a balance when exquisite yet intricate words flow from the mouth of someone who always displays an attitude of discontent for the simpler ways of a life never lived. (768)

How does a person who is considered to be an optimist who secretly consumes large quantities of hot chocolate, achieve a level of composure that exposes the myth of congruent pigmentations? (769)

Only by holding on to solemn attitudes that lack the pizzazz of an artichoke heart that must remain in seclusion until the applicable time to harvest asparagus has been announced to an anticipating world holding its collective breath. (770)

Will anyone who strives throughout their lifetime to maintain a proper attitude no matter how insignificant their objections are to untraceable ritualism, one day experience a complete break down in judgmental attitudes towards unredeemable impertinence? (771)

They will only experience a complete break down in judgmental attitudes when tension exists between the fusions of fissures that have developed in a life that makes a plausible effort to suspend the lawful attitudes of vibrant uncertainties. (772)

Can a blatant attitude of benevolence that is overexposed, someday be acknowledged as suitable for the liberation of unattainable ideas that have become thorns in the side of a foot that does not wear sandals? (773)

They will one day be acknowledged because bogus joy is sometimes intimidated by the same phony disturbing occupation that stalks the grandeur of transparent autonomous virtues. (774)

Why will lavish gifts that are given without any thought of celebrating the depths of despair, be swiftly returned to anyone who strives to live a life oppressed by a heavy load of predetermined malice? (775)

They will be swiftly returned because to give without ever wanting to get is a troubling paradox to those who lack the inability to assume the responsibility of desiring to become a role model for pranksters who will never become recognizable hoodlums. (776)

Who determines that the shameless life journey of a docile anchovy that swims aimlessly in a dangerous endless sea dreaming of one day becoming a humpback whale, is an inspiration to all that breathe and want to become more today than yesterday? (777)

A productive life that lacks an unattainable zeal that was never sought after or acquired by anyone who cared about such things and becomes a stumbling block to all well-wishers who enjoy snubbing everybody that always lands on their two feet. (778)

Is running around in circles easy to do if all you have ever known are squares. (779)

It is only easy if a person who always flip-flops has never come to grips with the heartfelt issues of those whose lives have been devastated by anyone who was overheard complaining about an acquaintance that could never stop griping about eating grapes that looked like apples. (780)

Are the important issues of life usually far more important to the issuers of the issues than to those who lack any interest in listening to the issuing of any issue? (781)

They are most important to the compassionate soul that feels the need to be needed by those who are needy and will someday be nominated for a one of a kind prestigious award that honors those select few who have chosen to be identified as needier than anyone who is needful. (782)

Is it possible for a character that becomes tarnished to never regain the luster of past glories unless it stumbles first into the heights of public embarrassment that once comforted by those whose inner strength was overpowered by an anemic disgruntled despot? (783)

Yes, and abundant opportunities will abound for anyone who leaves the cares of the world behind in an unmarked car that could have been stolen by someone who could not keep a promise. (784)

93

Can those who whine about murmuring even when they don't feel like it, appreciate intense resistance to new ideals that celebrate the diversity of significant contemptuous acts of imitative benevolence? (785)

No, because it is a difficult task to interpret ridiculously unimportant words that are meant to cause harm to those who proclaim peace without the sacrifice of explosive joy. (786)

Why does the legacy of a super ego's greatness lay only at the bottom of banged-up rusty old garbage can full of a lifetime of sour milk and rotten tomatoes? (787)

It is because valid authenticity that abdicates elegance without simplistic sophistication will one day succumb to the consequences of the actions of those who sought to do well without first being good. (788)

Is reaching the culmination of a journey the first stop in a lifetime of incomprehensible and inexhaustible questions for answers that shouldn't be understood by the simple minds of those who can comprehend certifiable weirdness? (789)

Actually, the first stop in climbing up a ladder before reaching the top is very similar to observing the pathway to the stars without a glimpse of imagination. (790)

Is it the nature of all things to seek the authenticity of genuine gestures of appreciation for prevailing winds of unclaimed scenarios? (791)

Yes, unless self–deception produces defenseless denial in those whose unmistakable source of awareness is vulnerable to the plight of those who have become weary from abandoning humanistic shame. (792)

Is a brief description always much better given in person, if the individual who is describing the event displays a lack of expertise that reflects the skillfulness of a repugnant uptight urbanite? (793)

It is much better given in person when undetermined phobias typically display a propensity to strengthen the disillusionment of despair and are able to first generate a need to narrowly define the contextual design that permeates from an unprovoked stillness. (794)

Can self-pity and defeatism only be overcome by the pugnacious purging of every thought that centers on the digestion of anything that contains chocolate from the memory of a mind of someone who also loves to eat dill pickles? (795)

It can only be overcome when emotional vacillation is sometimes spawned from the virus of superficiality that lays dormant for years in the lives of those who least expected to be attacked by primitive submicroscopic agents of change. (796)

Is it true that peculiar people who are really peculiar are really no different from those who seek the affirmation of significance from aliens who once visited the earth from the planet Zebu-nebula? (797)

It is only true when a deliberate thought is purposefully lodged firmly in an unassuming mind, and only those who know the secret art of mindless destabilization can find the lost memories that were once forgotten. (798)

Should the responsibility of molding the thoughts that shape the minds of our precious children, be left up to those who do not know how to facilitate the life-changing concept that will change the world known as *"The sporadic familiarization of complicated reflective analogies?"* (799)

The responsibility should be left up to those who concur that reasoning that is inspired by internal gastric irruptions, will usually pass in the night if left undisturbed by those who disregard proper etiquette when it applies only to someone other than themselves. (800)

Session 9

"Privileges that overshadow absurdity"

Will handling prosperity with a tranquil attitude, allow others in need to exhibit the indispensable sense of confidence needed to force those with adjusted attitudes to relinquish control of complete submissiveness? (801)

A relaxed attitude will only affirm that numerous exemptions are usually found within the dignity of exorbitant extremes. (802)

Is it true that sprinkled with a sense of poise is the individual whose unquestionable toughness always permeates the conversations of those who continually examine the physical nature of complex unreliable circumstances? (803)

No it is not true, because manipulated misinterpretations sometimes manipulate misguided idiosyncrasies that attempt to dominate every conceivable situation that might arise from illogical conclusions. (804)

Is the ultimate reward one that is subtle and without fear of being rejected by an overpowering commendation of specifics? (805)

It is only subtle to those who must always reflect on past reflections that fear the anticipation of seeing the reflected light at the end of a tunnel that has no name. (806)

Will ambitions whose roots are embedded in soil of despair ever be allowed to visit the precious memories of those who linger beneath the legacy of forgotten dignity? (807)

They will only be allowed to visit when the fear of competitive pressure by those who often stumble, is not a reason for someone to intentionally forget the real meaning behind vivid remembrances that once buckled under the immense critical criticism of inadequate resources. (808)

Why is it an often a marvelous thing to watch a flock of birds nestle snugly for the evening in a tree whose leaves glisten in the dew of a starlit night, after dropping presents from above throughout a day that should have lasted a week? (809)

It is because abundant opportunities abound for those who will earnestly take the time to sit down and listen to sounds that have no voice and endings, which require no story. (810)

Why is it that the only alternative available for an alternate view that can affect an abrupt change in a pathetic excuse for a stiff-necked society, is to allow the intensity of every moment to disintegrate into a momentous finale of ridiculous calmness? (811)

The motivation for this is that it should never be an unscrupulous idea for someone to agonize over something that was not even there in the first place. (812)

Is it possible that sometimes the path we take, leads us down a different road that few will travel because the universal road map that should have been created gave us directions to a place that not one person ever cared to find? (813)

It only leads those who must always contemplate the considerations of knowing that the thrill of success can only last for as long as supervision is superseded by mediocre excellence. (814)

Can trying to recover a latent truth from a closet of secrets past forgotten, lead to the discovery of a profound truth that cannot be displayed in a time that was never really real? (815)

It can't unless anyone that abdicates personal responsibility without first paying attention to the effects of periodic insomnia on dead birds, once again regains the respect of those who are always seeking renewed creativity. (816)

Will those who cling to ancient attitudes of euphoric serenity soon forget genuine authenticity that attempts to inspire spontaneous outbursts of oblivious outcomes? (817)

Yes it will soon be forgotten, especially when exhilarating moments of contemporary graciousness continually look for the adulation of reliable relevant benevolence that seldom becomes energized by unpopular superficiality. (818)

Why does a person who tries to avoid the unpleasantness of temporary discomfort never come to appreciate any aspect of unrestrained deceit that seeks to embarrass the exquisite circumstances of life? (819)

Those who are determined to despair over opportunities that always encouraged self-contempt, realize that trying to restore a good name without ever knowing the truth about pertinent information merely emphasizes the inadequacies of revealed interventions. (820)

Does duly noted hands-on experience allow those who do not know any better to actually learn to trust anyone who never knew that they never knew enough to not know too much? (821)

Duly noted hands-on experience allows a person who helps others to a greater personal awareness of the uniqueness of celebratory meekness to one day be rewarded for understanding the full spectrum of subsequent overconfidence. (822)

Can significant awareness sometimes confront the limited challenges that will help bring about the stabilization of old ideas that were once essential for the understanding of logical concerns? (823)

Yes they can always help bring about stabilization, because extraordinary impassioned appeals sometime intertwine with overlooked setbacks, which are unnoticed by those who favor ambitious aggressiveness. (824)

When is horrific situational disparity appreciated by persons whose intentions are suspect even if they were not suspected of following guidelines that could never be verified? (825)

They are only appreciated when an individual who strives to withstand the turmoil that directly affects personal mobility, follows the path of individual flexibility that was challenged by personal turmoil. (826)

Will the widespread normalization of forfeited pleasures ever come back to haunt incompetent leadership that never was satisfied with the containment of contained contentment? (827)

No, because the constant review of problematic pressures will lead to the complete break down in areas of the brain that is needed to understand the basic conceptual opportunities of illogical reasoning. (828)

Why do those who have failed to value the preposterous disposition of worthlessness, value mimicking a mocker? (829)

Because reasoning that penetrates the frailty of destitute hesitations, seldom finds significance in the hopelessness of sympathetic aversions to unorthodox animosity. (830)

Will resistance that constantly prevails in moments that often blindside the premonitions of the weary, lead back to the pinnacle of flippant adulation that so often evades the central themes of fluctuating articulations? (831)

Not at all, because that which is manifested in weakness will soon be overlooked by a strength that someday will rule the final oblivion of all things thought possible. (832)

Can an intellect that desires to manipulate the purposes found in the forgotten chambers of another person's broken heart discover only perfect rest while living in isolation among the crowded habitat of vested spectators? (833)

It can only find perfect rest when a need that attempts to hide the kindness of an individual who possess skillful clumsiness, desires to oppose outmoded and outdated habits that never are appreciated. (834)

Will a person who always believes in meaningful hesitations do what ever it takes to maintain a balance between things that last and lasting purposeful propositions that cannot be maintained? (835)

Yes, unless everyone who accepts the values of those who goals in life are never challenged by the big questions and are never able to celebrate the guaranteed satisfaction of accepting the rewards of those gifts that were presented without sincerity. (836)

Should any story that loses its meaning, become nothing but a useless conglomeration of wasted ink whose purpose for living will forever become haunted with the shocking truth that a tree in Georgia gave its life for nothing? (837)

No, because weird concepts that were first created by someone who was once stupid will force those who are wise in the literal sense to meditate upon words not yet created by the foolishness of differential insight. (838)

Will welcoming a stranger without first asking the name of another person's dog cause it to one day comeback to bite those who drink water from a glass without a first name? (839)

Not unless an individual who finds different ways of looking at the same solution creates additional problems that can only be found in the final solution. (840)

Does learning without ever living motivate some people to seek the approval of those who never lived without first being born? (841)

It does not motivate some people unless they believe that poor planning without ever considering the consequences for self-centered decisions will display to the world a life that can never again be trusted with the responsibility of deciding the outcomes for actions that struggle for significance. (842)

Is it true that people, who should travel down the mandatory path of total rejection, must make infinitesimal adjustments while always keeping in mind that tree limbs sometimes fall out of trees onto leaves without first names? (843)

No, because it is true that those who like to devour food and aspire to become finicky eaters will one day become what they eat while eating what they become. (844)

Are unclaimed affections sometimes saved in escrow by those who have placed on deposit pathetic attitudes that patiently wait for the eve of destruction? (845)

No one really cares, unless the exclusivity of diversified patterns of recent neglect is forced upon the weak that are becoming increasing stronger through the infestation of make-believe digitized uncensored supplemental enhancements. (846)

Is a commonplace theme that weaves its way through the fabric of time, always searching within the vastness of nothingness for its place of origin in the echoes of sublime serenity? (847)

No, because it believes that showing up for a special event just to eat the catered food is a despicable act that should be rewarded by those who have been punished by acute indigestion. (848)

Is a sly remark spoken in jest with a full grin sometimes much better received than a frown shared with others who can't even articulate the difference? (849)

It is only better received if it is void of any emotions and empty of any feelings for people who provide opportunities for others to manifest the profound futility of pointless playfulness. (850)

Why is it that apparently humanoids values are only esteemed by someone who is always trying to get in touch with the inner ideals of those who are no longer that which they knew they once were. (851)

The reason for this is that humanoids believe that just one word spoken with extreme intent, will change the results of ludicrous outlooks that bear no resemblance to vivid imaginative pictures full of diverse sensations. (852)

Will any excuse that does not have an attainable antidote often confuse those who are seldom confused by even the simplest form of enormous ideas? (853)

It will only confuse others if well-known patterns of adjustment can never replace the chauvinistic suppressions of subjugated exceptions. (854)

Does forging a trail into the wilderness of despair often lead an individual to a remote place where only virtue can coexist with those that reside in the village of mediocrity? (855)

It only allows an individual the ability to understand that the experience of a lesson lost, will never lose its willingness to find that which was misplaced but supposedly not totally found. (856)

Why does focusing only on good intentions bring things into focus that could not have been blurred without a considerable concerted effort? (857)

It brings only into focus the fact that those who too often wait for change must be careful to not hurry to discover the answers to make-believe questions. (858)

Will a person who makes bets on things they know nothing about, someday bring down irrational stupidity upon everyone who once placed their trust in guessing games? (859)

Yes, because hopeless avenues of solemn success may not be visible to anyone who stands tall without ever stooping to bend over. (860)

Is reaching the end of a final journey, only the first step in fulfilling dreams that did not have an ending but only a beginning? (861)

The first step of any journey is realizing that nothing that really matters most should not matter at all if what was gained only mattered to those whose treasured actions were accomplished for naught. (862)

When daylight eventually passes by in the morning, do some individuals care not to go home but only wait for a night that holds no fear of the midday sun? (863)

Things aren't what they ought to be because often others see visions of problematic differences that always make their way back into undesirable existence. (864)

Why does any wrong done in a timely fashion, place a large amount of unnecessary pressure upon those who have already paid the price for injustices that were never imagined or acted out in dreams? (865)

It places a large amount of undue pressure upon those who have hidden from every option that will never provide the answers needed to lament over wasted time spent wisely. (866)

Does not sanding off the rough edges always determine a smooth finish for those that can't tell the difference? (867)

It doesn't determine anything except that the anticipation of things that are about to happen may be unrealistic to a future to come that knows no limits but fixed boundaries. (868)

Will possibilities that provoke the pain of past hurts that are not yet healed always leave open wounds that can never be discouraged even when remembered by open thoughts? (869)

They leave open wounds because people who must answer every question with a question generally exhibit a predetermined mindset that refuses to believe anything except that which has been answered with an answer. (870)

Shall sobering thoughts that must nestle into the goodness of all that will soon disappear, ever appreciate the end results of fortunes soon to be realized? (871)

They must only nestle in private conversations that should never be repeated in the company of others who trust only in public displays of outward compassion that is never granted permanent sanctuary. (872)

Is it true that the individual who tries to manipulate every single solitary conversation is only trying to share feelings of tenderness that always negates the positive effectiveness of an overabundance of words? (873)

No, it is only true that prolonged provocative problems should never become a substitute for something that can never be properly interpreted. (874)

Does someone who does not comprehend the essence of inspired irritability ever appreciate treating others with impossible respect? (875)

It is usually never appreciated by unfounded allegations that were prepared with considerable deliberation and replaced by a cloud that has no direction. (876)

Why do unique indescribable challenges await those who endeavor to interpret the confusion of all embarrassments? (877)

They await those who endeavor to interpret the confusion of all embarrassments because diminished returns are a prized possession of any individual who abandons the covenant of disavowed degradation. (878)

Will every obligation that is entrusted to wishful thinkers withstand the test of microscopic futility that originates from numerous months of intense planning? (879)

Every obligation will only withstand the test of microscopic futility if it understands that every hour of everyday somewhere in the world a tree whispers the sweet songs of the grasshopper that often dreams of a life once forsaken by the north wind. (880)

Does the pitter-pattering of presumed ponderings often persuade those who dance for rain to scamper for cover into a building without a roof? (881)

It only persuades the individual who displays pathetic attitudes of persistent arrogance and reframes from singing silly songs that lack meaningless insight. (882)

Are hopeless neglect and infinite possibilities frequently contained in the wisdom of a beautiful sunflower that turns its face away from the southern sky? (883)

They are only contained in the purest form of stupidity that often hides itself within the confines of blind ignorance that might not remain undetected. (884)

Why do compliments that are intended to diffuse the tension of the moment often remain silent to thoughts of pleasant offenses that should not be deciphered? (885)

They remain silent because they understand that they must listen to the cries of the moment, or the moment will no longer hear the pleas of those who trust in self-denial. (886)

Why do persons who are always opposed to the disillusionment of inappropriate etiquette never see primitive originality? (887)

Primitive originality is never seen because an individual, who is opposed to the brevity of unspoken thoughtless dreams, always appreciates mundane humble beginnings. (888)

Why does an annoying odor often become a sweet aroma to those who smell the pits of peaches left to decompose on the groundless waste of inconsequential fruitlessness? (889)

It is because the sweet aroma of vindication is not based upon the truest form of authoritarian exoneration and will fail to materialize in a perfect world that is full of assimilated absolutes. (890)

Will steps that are taken without any deliberation into the reasons behind indirect intentions, fall flat on a dirt floor of polished straw? (891)

They will fall flat on a dirt floor of polished straw only when a docile dingo redirects the paths of anyone who forgets the future while meditating on the past that cannot be discovered. (892)

Should something that could have never been, be allowed to become anything that someone else would really not have cared to even notice? (893)

It should never be allowed to become anything else because to determine nothing will only control the outcome of anything that is resolute. (894)

Should an unconcerned perpetrator of justice one day be rewarded for the actions of all who could not respect the individuality of the common earthworm? (895)

The unconcerned perpetrator should only be rewarded while attempting to laugh harder at seemingly absurd remarks that lesson the blow of direct complaints not given to others who are never surrounded by existing circumstances. (896)

Is it possible for mental capabilities to outlast the brains of those who know not to do with much of anything with something that once was considered? (897)

It is possible, if the straight path of a narrow way is only crooked to those who cloak their dreams in the anguish of clandestine disbelief. (898)

Can a hug without the warmth of a coldness that will not be denied, last longer than the dew that becomes lost in its own reflection? (899)

It will only last longer when hate without anger lingers in the limbo of a mind full of malice far from the pleasure of the purest greed. (900)

Session 10

"The simplicity of dismal pleasantness"

Can advantageous beginnings thrive next to the by-product of recurring occurrences? (901)

It can only thrive when complete and utter chaos lives in the hearts and minds of undiscovered hermits who exist in a place where nothingness can only survive. (902)

Is the ridiculous nature of natural ridicule only found in remote isolated areas where lizards bark at the moss in trees? (903)

It is only found where a person who stares at the stars will never be blinded by the particle density that cannot be calculated in time worth managing. (904)

Why is something new and someone old never adequate for any situation that must be terminated without first disagreeing to agreeable terms? (905)

It is only adequate when absolute discretion actively endorses the uniqueness of all non-misleading reservations. (906)

Why is any good idea only as good as its goodness will not allow? (907)

It is only as good as its goodness will not allow because pertinent petitions that try to confuse a country full of devoted fakes, will often confuse the intellect of a tiny goldfish with that of a cricket. (908)

Why does selecting a friend whose sole purpose in life is to pluck and devour a green plum, make about as much sense as the definition for the word plick? (909)

It makes only sense if ignorant stupidity lives in the mindless vacuum of transparent minds whose common sense has left for a winter that will never exist in a past that was never near. (910)

Should honest integrity that sincerely seeks the respect of others who are respected first, consult with those who least expect the unexpected acceptance of accepting full responsibility for something that came from nothing? (911)

No, because some people walk the earth in a cloud of mindless density and refuse to function with any sense of maturity that is displayed and revealed in the brain of a parasite. (912)

Is a pathetic neurosis a disease most commonly diagnosed in individuals who eat acorns from a tree that does not bare nuts? (913)

Yes, and only a weak mind should follow the strong heart of a person who puts ketchup on a tomato and devours it with a straw. (914)

Will kindness that refuses to show respect to a breeder of Marmosets ever have an appreciation for attitudes not allowed beyond the point of observed absurdity? (915)

It will only have an appreciation when rain that falls between the cracks of time, puddles at the feet of infinitesimal souls. (916)

Why is it wise to beware of birds that whisper sweet melodies of unknown songs while they fly through the air without parachutes? (917)

It is wise to beware, because a wicked tyrant, who plans with wise council to unleash a detestable evil upon those who await doom, will one day soon be forced into isolation by a mob that only listens to the pleasant sounds of blended rubbish. (918)

Is it possible for unthinkable confidence that will soon replace the emptiness created by an uncontrollable tongue, to yearn for the day that opportunities abound for those who can actually speak? (919)

It will only be possible if intensive alternate interventions improve the infrastructure of a global curriculum in which its members refuse to discuss the need for alternative solutions to worthless resolutions. (920)

Do difficult times usually bring out the best in make-believe attitudes that hibernate in months where they are needed least? (921)

They only bring out the best in make-believe attitudes when it is understood that the brain of a virtuoso is slightly more conceded than that of a stupid idiot who is smarter than a fool. (922)

Will listening to the advice from an egotistical geek cause an effect that will most likely infect anyone who has been affected by a geek? (923)

It can cause an infection only if smoke that follows an eastern path dissipates as it ascends into the glorious emptiness of oblivion. (924)

How can it be true that enduring rewards do not wait for those who ultimately linger by the roadside of an ordinary event that each day faces the unchecked reality of useless expectations? (925)

The reason it is true is because people who never have visions will usually invent carefully worded antidotes that normally replace the common sense approach of failing with options. (926)

Is it probable that only a vapor found in the mist of a fog can find its way back into the midst of a haze that will never depart from the suspended particles of an unknown liquid? (927)

It is probable just as it is mandatory that any person who refuses to think should be sent immediately to a world where thoughts once lived in harmony with new ideas that could never be revealed by words that never should have been spoken. (928)

Is it possible that once something is repeated again that anything that could have been repeated in the future will never be repeated? (929)

Yes it is possible, because one less or one more really doesn't matter if what is more could never be less. (930)

Why is a waste of time only wasted when time is spent worrying about when the clock will once again return to a time well spent? (931)

It is only wasted because the generalization of situational conceptualization is purposeful disregarded when those who proclaim the diversity of all deception misunderstand a belief. (932)

How is it possible that silliness flourishes in the depravity of a moment that cannot be desensitized? (933)

It flourishes because growing concerns of neglectful attitudes must never become a substitute for varying levels of assessments. (934)

Can useful offenses sometimes directly affect the achievements of progressive actualizations? (935)

It can only directly affect the achievements when the ability to demonstrate common sense is not communicated when a task is presented in a format of increased importance. (936)

Should routines that seek to practice repetitive habits be scrutinized by relative itemizations? (937)

They should never be scrutinized, because those decisions are actually independent of claimed standards that show a reluctance to maintain a low level of equalized importance. (938)

Can public knowledge become finicky when compared to changes within granular specific details? (939)

Public knowledge can only become finicky when a starting point attempts to find the conceptualized factors hidden within shared reflections. (940)

Will supplemental options ever become the functional mainstay of a community diversified by unattainable benchmarks? (941)

It can only become the functional mainstay of a community when a typical presentation that sparks a desire to practice practical knowledge, connects with the minds of those who ascend to the upper levels of ultimate kindness. (942)

Why must validity be verified in order to maintain a sense of calm that continuously monitors unexplained evidence? (943)

Validity must be verified because specific exemptions have no expectations when presented in public with repetitive base line items. (944)

Why is actually attainable progress frequently considered a casual reflection of cultural distinctive imaginations and known only by a select few? (945)

It is because actual attainable progress is often considered by those who strive to know the things that are known by a few and subdued by a distinct audience that must be revealed through time least spent. (946)

Are greater possibilities a useful aid when searching for results that should not be reported by an individual who lives to please a task that can never be completed? (947)

They are only a useful aid when they are combined with an active inner personalization, which is a powerful tool to use when trying to describe the classic detailed outcomes of possible filtered results. (948)

Does working together to perfect a necessity for accurate comparisons, seldom impart a perspective that reveals regulations that should not be discussed? (949)

Yes, because seldom seen are the things that could never be discovered while visiting places that could not possibly exist in the minds of those who once reverenced relevant gestures. (950)

Is silence often searched for in the places that one day will be revealed by a cold heart that beckons for a voice it cannot hear? (951)

Silence is searched for only when misconceptions often rise above the folly of awkward appearances that still remain when vanquished by the outer goodness of a blameless act of kindness. (952)

When must detrimental significance become the reason for living in a world fortified by the neglectful attitudes of blatant lies? (953)

It must never become the reason because hopeless devotion that is only focused upon the pleasures of wickedness yet to be determined, will often become the reason why others leave only to find another way. (954)

Why do some people live their lives for the untold shyness of laughter waiting to be revealed? (955)

It is because things that seem to be known are never exhausted by the patience of sincere sacrifice. (956)

Why should futile efforts always support those precious treasures that are the foundation of peculiar endeavors? (957)

They should support those precious treasures because however perplexing a situation might have become, always remember that reason is sometimes embarrassed by the few who seek the recognition of many determining factors. (958)

Is every other exception seldom inclusive of every part of maximized improvement? (959)

It is only inclusive of every part of maximized improvement when opportunities are continually searching for the impact of abundance on the lives of individuals who share the quality of secluded possibilities. (960)

Why is experiencing the pleasures of pleasant pleasantries often valued more than the momentum that was lodged in the smallest deviation? (961)

It is only valued more than the momentum that was lodged in the smallest deviation because who you were, is not who I am, if what I was, is no longer where you are. (962)

Is the pursuit of excellence a habit that has become the mindset of a continuous potential that has abruptly been abandoned in the midst of unprovoked circumstances? (963)

No, because enthusiasm is never contained by the emotions of expectation left to the reliability of any situation. (964)

Is it ever possible to develop an intuitive plan that can be realistically performed in haste by those who least expect to hear an ultimatum given by those who posses unexpected opportunities? (965)

It is only possible when dependable practices based upon timeless traditions never become misplaced in the hustle and bustle of collected thoughts left for dead. (966)

How is it possible for consolations that cannot be controlled, to collect the dust of particles that have no home but their own? (967)

Actually, it is not possible because maturity without a deep realization of expanded recollections often pretends to be something that it should never have become without first giving a suitable explanation. (968)

Is the only thing a person needs is what they never should have received in the first place? (969)

Nobody really knows except those who believe that relieving nervous anxieties sometimes brings about confusion into the lives of those that openly disappear when situations develop from sudden procrastination. (970)

Is being comfortable in any situation a difficult task to master when trying to hide from invisible circumstances that would never appear unless spoken about beforehand? (971)

It is a difficult to master because using not enough words during complex conversations sometimes is an embarrassment to those who find little comfort in knowing nothing about anything. (972)

Why is keeping an open mind in a closed environment difficult to imagine, if others who surround an event lack the abilities to admit to always answering dumb questions that were never appreciated? (973)

It is a challenging realization to imagine because maintaining a sense of calmness while forgetting to prepare for undeserved conflicts seldom benefits anyone except those who fail to deliver on promises that were never alive. (974)

Will limiting the limitations of those who have never had boundaries usually place undetermined stress on the one who finds treasures while looking for garbage? (975)

No, because a dirty glass and an empty cup have nothing in common with a fork that was once a spoon used for soup. (976)

Why should people beware of a spontaneous gift that contains conditional stipulations that cannot be returned to the sender, even if some individuals will never return calls that should never have been made? (977)

People must be aware of pride that continually attempts to evade a fall that will never realize the importance of holding onto things that are sometimes mindful but seldom speak their actual thoughts. (978)

Can an age of hope that has yet to be discovered ever be created by mere inventions from a mind whose resentments to determinations are still waiting to be discovered? (979)

Yes, because taking care of business without first knowing the outcome of what will be taken care of, is like never knowing what is recognized without first knowing what is assumed. (980)

Is it true that trying to escape a construct reality in a society that has a difficult time with divergent attitudes is only impossible for those that are always in contact with the makers of strategies that will not succeed? (981)

It is not true unless gathered insightful individuals who purpose in their hearts to believe in contrite complimentary remarks that have been categorically approved, find information that has been hid from the general populous for more than one year. (982)

Why does hiding a secret in private become a confusing experience for those whose only interaction with the public has been from behind a closed curtain on an open stage? (983)

It can become a confusing experience because an individual who gets so wrapped up in their own things without first analyzing the circumference of an invisible circle will also have difficulty discovering the radius of a square. (984)

Why is just showing up without really being there like living in a town without ever meeting one person who knows how to fish for cut bait? (985)

The only reason for this is that humor is essential when choosing the useful appetite for the food that will soon be devoured by the tasteless oracles of sudden bolts of energetic estimations. (986)

Are people who often lose their way really never lost while searching for what was never found by others who do not believe in the admiration of future lost ideals? (987)

They are really never lost because individuals, who see with their own eyes, are the same individuals who can only sense what their nose cannot smell. (988)

Could properly placed paranoia only be perfected when persistence is manifested in eyes that blink but will not twitch? (989)

It can only be perfected by a pragmatist who is neither prompt nor prepared and never be called upon to address those whose lives have been previously influenced by uncontrolled restraint. (990)

Do inner qualities often reveal to others the real purpose of a loner who is always trying to impress an inebriated person who has not had a drink? (991)

This is a possibility because a person who is seeking the intervention of independent dependability will usually be disappointed by events that took place at an earlier convenience. (992)

Does maintaining a sense of balance while denying the existence of equilibrium always confuse those who lack the proper judgment to not force an issue without first counting the cost? (993)

Maintaining a sense of balance while denying the existence of equilibrium always confuses individuals who only seek adulation from persons who will never experience the sounds of silence in a forest, while not being left alone. (994)

Does wishful thinking that is usually preceded by spur of the moment regressive behavior only lead to the destruction of appetites that won't digest words? (995)

No, because perseverance under momentary pressure will assure that no one will ever discover the desire to hide from things that can only be heard without much need for considerable thought. (996)

Will the reasoning behind any answer that is questioned without hesitation often reflect the thoughts of those who lack the ability to apprehend comprehension? (997)

It will only reflect the reasoning of those who find themselves void of any feelings and seldom find happiness from the pessimistic encouragement of insignificant others. (998)

Is striving to preserve the continuation of the greater good only contagious if diagnosed while swimming in a pool without water. (999)

It is only contagious if a person whose sole purpose in life is to impress anyone whose nightmares always bring comfort to individuals in need of resentment and are seldom taken away by anyone who always finds the need to reflect on natural superficiality. (1,000)

Will the individual who is never found ever need to find the need to be found in the first place? (1,001)

Only when this person becomes a caring individual and others see the person who long ago was once really somebody. (1,002)

Not the end of something that was never intended to be anything at all.

CPSIA information can be obtained
at www.ICGtesting.com
Printed in the USA
BVHW071924231118
533785BV00017B/408/P